DAILY HABITS OF TEA AND JOY

A Gentle Guide to Finding Everyday Joy
Through Tea, Gratitude & Mindfulness

ZAKIYYA ROSEBELLE

HAPPY ROSY DAY, CALIFORNIA

HAPPY ROSY DAY
San Francisco, California

Copyright © 2025 by Zakiyya Rosebelle

All rights reserved. Thank you for buying an authorized edition of this book and for complying with copyright laws by not reproducing, scanning, or distributing any part of it in any form without permission. You are supporting writers and allowing us to work hard to make our books available to readers.

Limit of Liability/Disclaimer of Warranty: The information in this book is provided for informational purposes only, without any warranty of any kind. It is sold with the understanding that the author and publisher are not engaged in rendering legal, financial, medical, or other professional services. This book does not diagnose, treat, or cure medical or mental health conditions. The author and publisher shall have neither liability nor responsibility to any person or entity with respect to any loss or damage caused, or alleged to be caused, directly or indirectly,
by the information in this book.

ISBN 979-8-9936908-0-3

Cover & Interior Text Design by Zakiyya Rosebelle.

For My Little Loves

♥

Contents

The Cup that Changed Everything	1
Blooming from Within: Loving Yourself	10
The Rhythm of Daily Joy	28
Tea Time: A Romance to Boost Joy Every Day	41
Joy as a Daily Practice	51
A Morning Routine that Changes Everything	66
When Love Becomes a Daily Practice	73
Tea, Scones, and the Joy of Being Together	84
Embrace the Sunset: A Calm Evening Routine	93
The Cup That Powers Habit	99
Your Cozy Corner of Joy	112
The Teapot of Gentle Reminders	124
The Gratitude Habit	130
The Habit of Appreciating the Little Things	139

Daily Gratitude Affirmations	145
Steep. Savor. Soften.	150
Where Does Joy Hide on Mondays?	165
Daily Habits of Joy Calendar	173
Build a Life You Love	185
Creating Room for Joy	195
Is There a Place Where Joy Grows Wild?	203
When Joy Feels Far Away	209
Tea Parties and Tickle Fights	215
A Little Habit to Heal the Heart	232
Gratitude as Your Guide Through Hardships	239
A Daily Cup of Kindness, Warm and Sweet	249
The Beauty You Almost Missed	264
Daily Habits, Warm Sips, Joyful Living	274
Where Joy Grows Wild	278

Introduction

The Cup that Changed Everything

The setting sun paints the world with a warm, golden glow on this pleasant summer's day. The melody of the day is slowly fading away, and the world is drifting into calm. Bright lights gleam through my kitchen window, giving you a glimpse of the color and charm glittering inside. The warm and aromatic scents of cinnamon, nutmeg, and clove infuse the air as a pink pot of black tea brews on the stove. *Beep. Beep. Beep.* The oven's alarm goes off. The pumpkin scones are ready. A heavenly aroma of sweet pumpkin and rich spices escapes when I open the oven door. As I breathe in the delicious air, I lift the pan with my tea-themed oven mitt and place it on the yellow trivet resting on the table. I set the steamy pieces of scones on a serving plate adorned with pretty illustrations of pastries and cakes.

Welcome to my tearoom-themed kitchen. A cool breeze gently blows the pink ruffle curtains hanging along the sliding door. I gingerly carry my most beloved teapot and the warm scones to the backyard, full of life and under the reign of flowers, fruits, and butterflies. Here, the birds are guests, and they feast on gourmet food in a cute house of their own in the tree. Strands of fairy lights are draped from the branches of a maple tree. Beneath it sits a white table aglow with twinkling tealight candles. Little lanterns in pink, yellow, green, and blue dangle from tree branches like chandeliers.

A whimsical, heart-shaped tea set is the jewel of my tabletop. The dainty little heart-shaped porcelain cups—in pretty pastel shades—add a quaint touch to my tea table. It was this very tea set that inspired my journey to the gentle art of living well through tea, love, and daily beauty. My, how very picturesque and lovely it all is! Immersed in magic, my garden—blooming with color and fragrance—is a most enchanting sight.

Ding dong; the doorbell rings. There is a brief pause, and thirty seconds later it rings again, this time more insistently. It's tea time, and I have company. The wind carries the subtle fragrance of flowers married with the smell of pumpkin, spice, oh yes, and the sweet vanilla scent of candles. The gilded glow that brightens up my soirée slowly fades, and dear companions and I delightedly sip tea until sunset.

HOW I DISCOVERED HABITS

I have a passion for tea and a love for finding and spreading joy. Gladly, the two often go hand in hand, and for this, I am grateful. Long ago and not far away, I grew up in a Fijian household where I had the pleasure of tasting tea at the age of two and enjoying teatime with loved ones at six. Ever since then, tea has been an integral part of my family's day. Each morning, we have been filling our home with its warm aroma, giving us a sense of calmness, and at the same time, energizing us to start the day. Tea is the jewel that is at the center of the most joyous memories that adorn my heart.

Afternoons brought with them a moment to take pleasure in the little things—time to enjoy with family and an opportunity to pause and notice the beauty around me. A cup of tea, the company of loved ones, and a calm moment filled with lighthearted chatter. Tea became more than just a cozy drink; it became a lifestyle and a grounding experience that filled my afternoons with gratitude, connection, and happiness. I began weaving this delightful practice into my routine, and before long, it turned into a source of daily joy and a habit that nourished my spirit. It led to the creation of The Tea & Joy Method: a gentle system for designing joy into ordinary days.

Over time, I gradually discovered that tea carried more than its health benefits and a moment of calm. The boiling water, the rising steam, the steeping leaves, and the slow first sip became a soothing rhythm that gently encouraged the changes I wanted to make. It flowed naturally, with the idea that small, consistent routines help budding habits blossom. It was then that I realized my morning cup of tea had become a warm haven of mindfulness, gratitude, and quiet personal growth.

When a new intention is linked to something familiar and comforting like teatime, it becomes easier to return to. Though not every chapter in this book delves into the science of habit formation, in The Cup That Powers Habit, I share an approach I've lovingly shaped over the years and often pass along to my clients. It touches on a habit science framework, offering a deeper look at how small changes can create lasting impact. The remaining chapters are a part of The Tea & Joy method, offering gentle guidance, inspiration, simple tools, and repeatable practices for finding and creating joy in the ordinary moments that shape our days.

WHY I WROTE THIS BOOK

I would like you to know that you don't have to change your entire life to feel better. You just need to build one good habit at a time—and maybe brew a warm cup of tea.

According to research, half of our tendency toward happiness is genetic, and a portion is attributed to our circumstances. The rest is a result of good habits that, when consistently practiced, can lead to significantly improved circumstances over time.

I want to create value with my life, inspiring and uplifting others to live better. Helping others is one of the daily habits that boosts my sense of happiness and well-being. If even one beautiful moment blooms in your day from this inspiration, an unspeakable gladness will fill my heart.

This book is not a substitute for therapy or medical care. It offers practical perspectives drawn from research, professional experience, and lived insight. I am not a healthcare professional and am not giving any type of advice. I want to share with others how small shifts transformed my life. This book is filled with glimpses of my personal journey. It holds the positive practices and joyful routines I embrace to beautify each day. Blending cozy storytelling with practical, habit-shaping tools, this book invites you to build a life you love—one quiet, nourishing moment at a time.

Throughout my life, I often wondered if there is a place where joy grows wild. As I began cultivating positive habits over the years, I also set out on an exciting quest—not to find love, not to find myself. I was looking for a joy that endures, steady and unwavering, through all of life's seasons. The kind that lives in small moments and gentle practices—in the pages of a good book, in the company of family and friends, in the delight of an afternoon with tea.

I wandered through tearooms across the world. From the rain-washed windows of London tearooms to the mosaic-tiled courtyards of Istanbul, I searched not for a big discovery, but for something simpler. I longed for the kind of joy that would bloom within me, no matter what challenges I faced, growing deeper and more radiant with time. The kind of joy that, like wildflowers, grows wherever it can—untamed, beautifully resilient, surprising you in places you'd least expect.

I wrote this gentle guide with the hope that it brings a little more warmth and inspiration into your day. Within these pages, you'll find simple practices—like empowering affirmations, mindful moments, and small, joyful habits—that I hope resonate with you. Have you ever experienced that one moment when something small brightens your whole day? That's the kind of shift I want you to experience here. With tools for everyday joy, including the Teatimely Habits Method, the Daily Habits of Joy Calendar, joy menu, and more, I hope that you find something that sparks meaningful change, big or small. If even one of these little shifts brings more joy or peace into your life, I'll consider it a success.

HOW THIS BOOK WILL BENEFIT YOU

Would you like to know where joy grows? Are you ready to find that one small yet powerful practice that can help you live with more presence, peace, and contentment? *Daily Habits of Tea and Joy* is a gentle and transformational guide to feeling better every day and finding joy in your daily life.

Through small, doable habits—steeped in tea, love, gratitude, and mindfulness—you'll learn how to bring beauty to your mornings, calm to your evenings, and more meaning to your everyday life.

Whether you are starting a new chapter, feeling overwhelmed, or simply craving more connection with yourself, this book is your kind companion on the journey to building a more joyful, intentional way of being—one tiny habit at a time. You have the power to create moments of joy and beauty every day—starting today, starting here.

Your mind is like a canvas. You are the artist, and the paintbrush is in your hand. You can choose the colors to use and the images to paint. You can create a beautiful masterpiece if that is what you envision. I would like you to paint two pictures with me today. This exercise is an important part of understanding your outlook in life.

No matter what your artistic ability is, you are encouraged to create these two paintings. Sit by yourself with a palette of paint, paper, and a paintbrush. If you do not have paint, then color pencils or crayons will do.

On the first piece of paper, capture all of the unintentional thoughts and feelings that are on your mind at this moment. Express everything as accurately as you can by using cheerful, upbeat colors for positive thoughts. Use gloomy colors to depict the negativity you feel. Portray all of the hidden thoughts that indirectly affect you. Let this painting dry, and with the bright, cheery color palette in hand, begin creating the second painting. It should reflect the life you wish to lead.

Now, place the two paintings you have created side by side, comparing them. How can you make your life look more like the promising version in the second painting? Add happiness habits to your routine, paying attention to them, cultivating them, and practicing them every day. Hang the second painting on the wall. Let's set out on a beautiful journey during which we will pause, pour, and savor the beauty and joy in the little things.

I

Blooming from Within: Loving Yourself

I am of the opinion that true love cannot fully flourish without the gentle affection one bestows upon oneself. I come from a family that left their humble abode in search of a better life, facing almost every challenge one can think of. Growing up in an underprivileged town overflowing with disorder and lacking in aspiration, I experienced pain and overcame many of the challenges you may have also faced in your life. Yet this is a positive, uplifting book, so it is only fitting that I focus on beautiful thoughts, and I dearly hope you will welcome them.

I will share, though, that most of my life has been spent without the friendship of a kindred spirit. A misfit, shy and reserved, a little nerdy and very enthusiastic, the other kids always perceived me to be rather peculiar. I felt my first shove of animosity in kindergarten, and it persisted on and off all the way through high school. I spent a lot of time alone—playing, writing stories, and dreaming. This deep friendship with myself helped me cultivate lasting self-compassion. I love myself, and you should love yourself, too. We are all worthy of kindness and fondness, and it all starts with fostering a deep, enduring love for ourselves.

Happiness is an accumulation of small moments of beauty and joy. Weave small habits of love, gratitude, and joy into your daily routine to boost the number of uplifting moments in your day.

Love is a precious gift that inspires us to see the beauty around us, and for that, we should be grateful. And, if love is the most valuable gift worthy of gratitude, then surely, loving yourself is invaluable. Powerful and transformative, cherishing yourself fully has the magic to change the way you see the world.

When you view life through the lens of self-love, a rainy day becomes an opportunity to indulge in cozy contentment with a warm cup of tea and a comfy blanket. A moment of solitude becomes a moment of peace. An exhausting day becomes an opportunity to nourish yourself through self-care. A difficult time becomes a lesson and an opportunity to grow. Your heart becomes a bright, sunny garden where you plant flowers of love and kindness for yourself and others, enriching your life with beauty and fragrance.

Research suggests that cultivating self-love can help improve your physical and emotional well-being, increase self-esteem, and have happier relationships with others. It is about accepting who you are and celebrating your uniqueness, respecting yourself, and practicing self-compassion. When you learn to find beauty in your own being, you open your eyes to the beauty around you.

Has anyone ever told you that you should be more like somebody else? I have been told that I need to be richer, louder, better, more outgoing, and even less thin. Yet, there is no guarantee that someone richer is happier, someone louder does not cry silently when in solitude, and someone "better" is kinder. A person with a fuller body is not necessarily healthier, either. So, when the world tells us to be someone else, let us stand firmly in defiance by loving who we are and nurturing ourselves so that we may radiate with joy from within.

When we truly love ourselves, we can plant the seeds of all other loves—familial, romantic, platonic. What we can give to others is a reflection of the flowers we nurture within our own heart's garden. For a heart that has known its own compassion, kindness, and reverence can feel inspired to water the roots of all other loves.

It is important to understand that self-love is not about feeling good about yourself during a particular moment or under certain circumstances. Honoring your heart and soul is not loud, boastful, or pretentious. It is quiet, it is gentle, it is personal. It is about developing a deep sense of self-worth that remains strong, regardless of external circumstances. When you love yourself unconditionally, you feel more empowered to face life's challenges. Not being hindered by self-doubt can help boost confidence. You may gain motivation to pursue your goals, have healthier relationships, and contribute positively to the world around you.

Cultivating self-love takes time and perseverance, and of course, there may be days when your persistence wanes, but remember your painting? Recall the scene of merriment you captured with crimson and lemon-yellow paint, so pleasantly cheerful. Being able to make this vision a reality can make all the effort worthwhile. So, without a moment's hesitation, let's begin this journey. With an open heart, free from any judgment, celebrate yourself regularly. Aim to make self-compassion a daily practice. Forgive yourself sincerely.

Dedicate time to nurturing self-love every day with small intentional practices.

Celebrate yourself today. Self-love begins with accepting yourself as you are and embracing all of the qualities that make you, *you*. Your strengths, capabilities, weaknesses, and imperfections—all perfectly create the masterpiece you are. Instead of worrying about being a certain way, be true to who you are and let your strengths shine. Tell yourself, "I am enough, just as I am. I embrace my unique qualities." Self-love is when you learn to feel comfortable in your own skin, accepting your fortes and your flaws as a part of your journey.

You are adorned with the beauty of blooming flowers—roses, orchids, and lilies—each one reflecting the unique qualities that make you shine. Within you sparkle precious gems: the emerald of your kindness, the sapphire of your wisdom, and the garnet of your resilience. And at the core of it all is your radiant heart, a brilliant diamond that lights up everything around you. You are a wonder in every sense, deserving of celebration. Mark today's date on your calendar, and dedicate this day to honoring the magnificence of *you*.

Your personality, skills, and physical attributes are unique to you. Your distinctive qualities set you apart from everyone else in this world. Your physical features give a face to the amazing soul that dwells within. You are special, my dear friend, and today I would like you to identify your glories and gifts. Write them down in your journal and read them every day until they are etched in your heart.

> I bake the best scones.
> I am a fun-loving person.
> I am smart and hardworking.
> I am compassionate.
> I am a good cook.
> I am a good listener.
> I am creative.
> I take care of my family.

If you're hesitant to start noting your strengths, I would be happy to help you get started. The following paragraph might look like a hodgepodge of words, but it is a list of qualities one may possess. Circle the ones that describe you.

Funny Sweet Entertaining Smart Creative Artistic Kind Compassionate Friendly Genuine Cheerful Good-hearted Diligent Mindful Loving Romantic Devoted Hardworking Nurturing Fun Energetic

Optimistic Generous Personable Caring Religious
Strong Ambitious Polite Open-minded Respectful
Spiritual Peaceful Giving Positive Patient Modest
Stylish Honest Cultured Grateful Ethical
Responsible Loyal Supportive Persevering
Confident Rational Helpful Forgiving Courageous
Productive Family-oriented Practical Happy
Empathetic Disciplined Adventurous Creative
Resourceful Elegant Wise Beautiful Thoughtful
Playful Calm Joyful Active Quirky

Now that you've acknowledged your glittering qualities, of which you should be proud, the hour has arrived for a celebration to be held in your honor. Having recognized your merits, you are ready to celebrate your day. What marks a special occasion in your home—a cake, a favorite drink, and flowers? Head to your local grocery store and pick up your favorite dessert, and buy yourself flowers. Upon returning home, brew your best tea, lick the foamy cream off the scrumptious dessert, and marvel at your beautiful flowers. If someone asks what the occasion is, tell them this is your day.

Self-celebration is a wonderful, tiny habit that nourishes the soul. Recognize the greatness within you, applauding your achievements, no matter how small. Praising successes—whether it's reaching a goal, learning something new, or overcoming a challenge—fosters a sense of satisfaction. It strengthens the belief that you are deserving of love and respect. When you recognize your accomplishments, you reflect on all of your capabilities, boosting your self-worth. Acknowledging your growth and achievements helps you affirm to yourself that you are worthy of appreciation and recognition.

EMBRACE SELF-COMPASSION

Be gentle with yourself. In loving ourselves, we can help create a more compassionate world that begins within our own precious hearts. A small yet mighty way to encourage self-love is through self-compassion. Learn to be more understanding and kind to yourself, treating yourself with the same care that you would offer a loved one. When you make a mistake or face failure, respond with gentleness. Try giving yourself empathy instead of judgment. Remind yourself that everyone is human, and everyone can experience difficulties and disappointments at some point in life. After all, life is about learning from your mistakes and growing stronger and wiser. Replace self-criticism with kindness towards yourself.

This shift is a big step toward embracing yourself as your most caring friend.

View yourself with warmth and empathy. Smile at yourself when you look in the mirror. Don't worry about looking a certain way, because you are lovely the way you are. Shift your gaze toward your natural beauty and your most attractive features. If you frequently stare at yourself in the mirror to search for flaws in your appearance, it might be to your advantage to reduce the number and visibility of mirrors in your home. Besides, mirrors fail to capture all your beauty, especially when you, your toughest critic, are appraising what you see.

If you seek a guarantee that your appearance is clean and tidy, then allow yourself a glance a handful of times between the morning and night. Yet, there is no need to seek reassurance about your beauty. Without a doubt, you are still just as beautiful as you were the last time you checked. And when you do happen to sneak a look, let the mirror reflect your goodness. Train your eyes to look past your exterior and see the skills, capabilities, kind acts, and good qualities that are safeguarded by this body of yours.

If you are trying to lose weight so you can fit into an outfit you used to wear, donate it. The timeworn garment is no longer good enough to hold the great qualities that you have developed throughout the years. Don't try to be the person you were back then, because you have grown a lot and come a long way. Be grateful for the experiences that have shaped who you are today. Turn your attention away from who you are not or what you don't have, and instead celebrate the beauty and abundance that exists in your life.

Give yourself a break. Become kindhearted and patient with yourself. Offer yourself some space to make mistakes. When you try something and do not meet your goals, remind yourself that it is okay. Positively communicate with yourself, gently reminding yourself that every disappointment brings an opportunity to learn something new. Making mistakes, realizing that you can do better, and taking the initiative to correct them is an enriching process. Life is about learning and growing. Every act of self-embrace, no matter how small, can transform you as a person.

Open your heart, and forgive yourself. Holding onto regrets or past burdens can prevent you from fully loving yourself. Offer yourself forgiveness for the mistakes you made yesterday and the ones you might make tomorrow. Missteps are an inevitable part of your journey, of everyone's journey. They do not define who you are, nor do they determine your worth. Love yourself enough to free yourself from self-imposed guilt and the negative emotions associated with mistakes of your past. Take something valuable from each experience. Writing down what you learned can bring clarity and growth. Try to see it from a different perspective so that you know, it did in some way, help you blossom into the strong and amazing person you are today.

It is finally time to forgive the child who didn't know better. Forgive the adult who failed. Forgive the heart that loved the wrong person. Forgive the soul that got lost. To love oneself is to forgive oneself and not underestimate one's abilities. It means not giving up on oneself and not abandoning one's pursuit of personal growth and happiness. Self-love is to cry without shame, to lose without breaking, to stumble without self-condemnation, and to fail without giving up. It is to rise, not out of fear of what others may think, but simply because you believe in yourself and want to try again.

DAILY HABITS OF SELF-LOVE

Prioritize small, intentional acts of self-love every day. Start each morning with a statement expressing one you thing you love about yourself. If you are having a busy day, then pause and take a break to nourish yourself.

Whether you take a light stroll or enjoy a tasty, nutritious meal, little acts of care are essential to one's well-being. Promise to do something nice for yourself every week. In doing so, you remind yourself that you deserve love and kindness, too. Whether you spoil yourself with a small gift, a treat, a favorite meal, or a nice experience, do so fondly, because you are worth it.

Strengthen your self-love with positive self-talk. When we criticize ourselves with negative self-talk, such as calling ourselves incompetent, inadequate, or unworthy, we unknowingly harm self-love. Since our thoughts can impact our feelings and our behavior, it's important to think well of ourselves. Reframe negative thoughts by pausing briefly and taking a moment to determine whether the thought is based on fact or reality. Chances are that they are not. Show yourself the same warmth and gentleness you offer others. When negative thoughts arise, gently replace them with affirmations of love and understanding. Practice empowering yourself regularly with positive self-love affirmations to boost self-esteem and discourage negative self-talk.

SELF-LOVE AFFIRMATIONS

- I accept myself for who I am.
- I am strong.
- I am enough, just as I am.
- I am confident.
- I believe in myself.
- I have everything I need to succeed.
- I forgive myself for my mistakes.
- I am capable of achieving my goals.
- I am worthy of love and respect.
- I deserve compassion, especially from myself.
- I am growing and learning every day.
- I am ready to let go of what no longer serves me.
- I give myself permission to grow and develop.
- I learn something from every experience.
- I love the person I am and the person I am becoming.
- I have the power and skills to do incredible things.
- I am worthy, whole, and complete as I am.
- The world needs my light, and I let my light shine bright.
- I don't need validation from others to know how good I am.
- I give myself permission to feel this way without judgment.

- ♥ I contribute beautiful things to this world, even if they are small.
- ♥ I strive to do my best every day, and that's enough.
- ♥ I am patient with myself as I go through this wonderful journey of life.

Repeating self-love affirmations daily can help you shift your focus to the beauty and strength within you. With time and perseverance, self-love can become a habit, one that transforms the way you view yourself and the world around you.

> **SIP OF INSPIRATION**
> Write uplifting messages and self-love affirmations, and stick them in places where they'll brighten your day.

Nurture self-worth. The greater your knowledge and skills, the more reasons you have to recognize and to celebrate yourself. What if you tried improving upon your weaknesses and dedicating time to developing your strengths? Let your gifts empower your self-esteem.

Think about ways to expand your intellectual horizons. You could read books, take courses, or attend workshops. Listen to audio books or podcasts while you cook or during your commute. There is a lot that can be learned through exploration. To develop your interest in history or art, take a trip to a museum or gallery. The more you know and are capable of doing, the greater your self-worth can be. One should be kind enough to allow oneself the opportunity to nurture capabilities, build skills, explore passions, follow dreams, and flourish.

Engage in activities that bring you joy. Remind yourself about your competency often by reflecting on your accomplishments and skills. Do the things you excel in so you that can feel good about yourself. In order to boost your confidence, consider sharing your talent with others. Take part in a contest doing something you excel in so that you can exhibit your flair and experience the pleasure of being acknowledged. If you're good at things like baking, cooking, or handcrafting goods, for example, you might share the things you make. Take pictures of your creations, and show it to others.

Create boundaries that protect your peace and personal growth. Self-love may involve setting healthy boundaries with others to protect your energy, time, and well-being. Learn to say no when something doesn't serve you, whether it's a request that drains your energy, a toxic relationship, or any situation that compromises your well-being. Never give anyone permission to bring you down, for how we let other people treat us is but a reflection of our love for ourselves. Self-love requires establishing limits to show respect and care for yourself and your needs. Prioritize your well-being without feeling guilty or overstretched. Healthy boundaries are an important way to preserve your mental and emotional health while honoring your beliefs and values.

Surround yourself with uplifting people. You are blessed with a beautiful life; it is enriched with plenty of thoughtful and supportive people. Preserve the positivity you work hard to achieve by limiting negative influences. On your self-love journey, avoid creating space for toxic people or situations. Negative or unsupportive relationships can drain your energy and hinder your progress toward self-love. Love yourself, and honor your right to a joyful life. Don't allow the opinions of others to cause you distress or question yourself. You know exactly what kind of person you are. Love your life enough to protect it from the disagreeable impact of harmful people.

Focus on nurturing the meaningful relationships in your life. Surround yourself with positive and loving people who support your goals, uplift you, and empower you to focus on the good things. Think about the people in your life, determine how they impact your well-being, and understand how they affect your love for yourself. Good company will encourage your personal growth, reinforce your sense of worth, and help strengthen your confidence. It's important to have a supportive and caring community, as it creates a safe space where you can express yourself authentically, without fear of judgment. Connect with the people who make you happy regularly, even if it means just sending over a quick text message.

Whenever you find yourself questioning your worth, remember that you have been a miracle since the day you were born. Always have faith in yourself. The conflicts you face in life and in relationships are tests. Overcoming these adversities with patience can help you realize your full potential, empowering you to emerge as your most marvelous self.

Self-love is about accepting yourself as you are, unconditionally. It involves celebrating everything that makes you marvelous, and letting your good qualities shine. Highlight the best in you, especially to yourself.

With love for yourself, you treat yourself with the same respect and kindness that you give to others. Practice self-compassion often, for this can help heal the hurt of your own heart and give you inspiration to plant seeds of kindness in the world.

There is no such person as one blessed with every charm of person and manner, for a unique set of flaws, vulnerability, and depth of heart is what makes one truly captivating. With a forgiving heart, embrace the entirety of your being—the hurt and the joy, the successes and the failures. For ultimately, it is a combination of both your imperfections and your magnificence that helps you reach the culmination of your true self and bloom into who you are destined to become. Remind yourself, as I often do, that even with our blemishes, we shine with a natural, resplendent beauty. By purposefully nurturing self-love daily, you are able to create a foundation of inner strength and joy that empowers you to live your best life.

2

The Rhythm of Daily Joy

In Istanbul, we wander through the Grand Bazaar, bustling with vibrant energy and a most enticing, exotic selection of goods. After several hours, I am ready for a serene steep of tea. My husband and I, excited to bask in the city's rich history and culture, one sip at a time, eagerly look around for an inviting café.

As we walk through the streets, my heart nearly skips a beat upon spotting a window display. Trays upon trays are piled high with freshly baked baklavas glistening with honey, in assortments I have never before seen. I marvel at the opulent spectacle of confections that I imagine were once enjoyed in Ottoman palaces. Heaping platters overflowing with jewel-toned Turkish delights in vibrant, juicy colors and indulgent flavors like rose, pomegranate, and chocolate ornament the sumptuous window display.

Hurrying inside, we sit at a table and order soul-soothing infusions with a random selection of sweets.

The waiter arrives with a silver tray and pours a steaming cup of Turkish çay (tea) for me, and my husband receives Turkish coffee. The deep amber liquid placed before me shimmers in the light, its aroma strong and sweet with apple. I smile as I lift my glass to my lips, the tulip-shaped cup delicate in my hands. As I take a bite of the kunafa, an utterly buttery pastry with cheese and warm, sweet syrup oozing out, I feel pure bliss. My husband, who is too busy to speak a word, luxuriates in the flavor of a pomegranate Turkish delight as it melts in his mouth.

We take pleasure in each bite as we exchange smiles and share laughter. Between sips of tea, the conversation wanders from our travels to the blessings that grace our lives—tea, exploration, and the unexpected places in which we seek and find joy. In Istanbul, with the historic skyline as our backdrop and the tea flowing generously, everything feels magical, even more magical than in Paris.

"Do you think we'll ever forget this tea date?" I ask, my mouth filled with sweets. My husband looks at me, his eyes sparkling with love for the city. "I think this is the one I'll never forget."

We finish our tea and pastries, lingering just a bit longer before leaving. As we walk hand in hand, I feel a deep sense of gratitude, as this city has revealed a distinct kind of joy to me. Steeped in enchantment, Istanbul has given us more than just afternoon tea—it gifted us a unique experience of flavors and culture, and a serene moment that we will cherish forever. This afternoon tea adventure taught me that contentment can be found nestled between tea leaves in unexpected places.

I discover that joy grows in the golden light in Istanbul, where a shopkeeper hands you a glass with a heartfelt smile, and you drink it calmly as the call to prayer echoes in the distance. You don't understand the language, but something in the warmth of the tea and the peacefulness of the moment tells you that you belong—even if just for now.

—— ✦ ——

Life is a journey of both beautifully mundane moments and fabulously unforgettable experiences. We experience simple joys and complex joys, and both are essential to our overall sense of well-being. Taking a stroll through a garden, spending time with loved ones, and traveling to a new place or enjoying the beauty of a different culture are among life's simple pleasures. These acts can make the day more beautiful.

Endlessly available are simple joys—those petite indulgences that bring contentment during the small moments you are gifted each day. Easily and abundantly found in ordinary moments and daily activities, there are many opportunities for you to seize simple joys every day, and it is for you to decide how many modest pleasures you wish to indulge in daily.

Fueling a richer sense of satisfaction and fulfillment are the complex joys—more grand or profound experiences that are noteworthy. Complex joys, which are more elaborate, might include achieving a significant goal, having a transformative experience, or building a meaningful relationship. Usually, these are not easily found or abundant in our everyday moments. The intricacies of complex joys often make them a bit more difficult to achieve. They are often multifaceted and require a greater investment of time, effort, and money.

Learning a new skill, completing a challenging project, making a long-term purchase, or experiencing a life-changing event can be profound. You can determine what kind of complex joy is meaningful for you, as what brings fulfilment can vary from person to person. For example, many people may consider buying a home to be one of their biggest dreams or an ultimate achievement. I, however, have never been in a rush to own a house. My foremost aspiration is to live with kindness and purpose, and to accumulate an extensive array of rare and everyday moments filled with the sensible joys of life.

Although they might require more time and resources, complex joys can be momentous. They have the potential to bring greater, long-lasting satisfaction and contentment. Getting your dream job, making a big purchase, learning new software, boosting confidence, and nurturing a beautiful relationship are all rather intricate and bring a different kind of joy. They may even consist of a blend of both positive and negative emotions. They may or may not last.

While complex joys can be immensely gratifying for a longer time, their acquisition may be temporary, leading to greater disappointment as they fade. Sadly, some very lovely relationships can fall apart. There might be a time when someone can no longer afford their dream home. There may be greater happiness when these kinds of joys bloom, and similarly, there may be greater distress when they wither away.

What makes simple joys so beautiful is that they are all around us, readily available, and found in everyday life. Although these are short-lived, there may be less disappointment when these fleeting moments of light pass. Overall, they still help us feel happier in life. While they often don't cost much money, we can enjoy many of life's simple, everyday luxuries for free. Strolling beneath the canopy of trees, sitting in your happy place at home with a warm cup of tea, and watching your favorite movie are small, fleeting moments of bliss. Yet these simple pleasures leave our lives a little deeper and our hearts a little fuller.

While both complex and simple joys might be essential to one's existence, there is a need to balance them to optimize happiness and meaning in life. Both can be essential to our overall well-being—with simple joys providing contentment in everyday life, and complex joys helping us find our life's purpose or greater meaning.

Perhaps, it may be appropriate to pursue one or two complex joys over a period of time—months, or years, depending on the nature of the potential joy. Since these require a greater commitment of time, energy, and resources, we don't want to pursue so many that we get swept away in this endeavor, denying ourselves the great pleasure of countless opportunities for simple joys.

Allow yourself the luxury of many quaint joys each day to stir a little sweetness into your routine. They are hidden in the small moments, waiting for you to find and enjoy. A warm hug, the company of a loved one, a tasty meal, and a relaxing bath—these are the little things that can be reveled in on even the most difficult of days. Delicately weave plenty of petite pleasures into your daily life. By developing the tiny habit of taking pleasure in life's simple joys, you can maximize the beauty and joy you experience regularly.

EVERYDAY JOYS TO WELCOME IN

1. Waking up to a new day in a familiar, comfy place.
2. A warm cup of tea, the fragrant steam rising gently.
3. Sunlight streaming through the window.
4. The joy of seeing a loved one's smile.
5. The adventure in the pages of a good book.
6. Lifting your spirits by uplifting someone through an act of kindness.
7. The satisfaction of a clean and organized space after tidying up.
8. Arranging fresh flowers in a vase.
9. Crossing off something on your to-do list.
10. The song of the birds greeting you in

the morning.

11. The first bite of your favorite treat.
12. The gentle embrace of the cool morning breeze.
13. A warm, cozy blanket on a chilly evening.
14. Wearing your favorite blouse or sweater.
15. The optimism of inspirational quotes and good news.
16. Cold water on a hot day.
17. Dancing to your favorite song.
18. Enjoying the comforting presence of family.
19. A delicious and nutritious meal that leaves you satisfied.
20. When the sun bathes our little world in a warm, golden glow.
21. A tranquil stroll through nature.
22. The excitement of working on a fun, creative project.
23. The feeling of your stress dissipating during a warm, relaxing bath.
24. A heartwarming hug.

25. The ease of watching a favorite TV show while sipping a warm cup of comfort.
26. The joy of planting a seed and watching it grow.
27. Sitting quietly and listening to the sounds of the world around you.
28. The life-changing magic of sharing laughter with your favorite people.
29. Marveling at the beauty of the sky painted in shades of pink, blue, and orange during sunset.
30. The contentment of a peaceful evening spent enjoying a pastime.
31. The glee of trying something new.
32. The sound of rain and its promise of rejuvenation.
33. The pure and free-spirited laughter of children.
34. The quiet moment before sleep, when the world is still and peaceful.
35. The joy of playfulness and doing something fun.
36. Settling into a neatly made bed.

37. The feeling of gratitude that blossoms when you count your blessings.
38. The tranquility of a moment enjoyed alone and free.
39. The night sky twinkling with stars.
40. The satisfaction of completing a puzzle.
41. Change of seasons, and the colors, climate, and little joys they bring.
42. Feeling grass or sand beneath your bare feet.
43. The pleasure of biting into a luscious fruit and tasting sweetness.
44. The serenity of a quiet morning with a cup of tea, steeped in positivity for the day ahead.
45. The joy of writing on pretty stationery.
46. The beauty of a vibrant garden with flowers and roses in full bloom.
47. The comfort of a light, airy fabric on a hot day and a warm, cozy fabric on a cold day.
48. The gentle glow of fairy lights twinkling in the evening.

49. The feeling of success after working hard on a task and completing it.
50. The warm and welcoming smell of freshly baked bread.
51. The sound of water cascading down a waterfall or small fountain.
52. The excitement of a trip or adventure.
53. The fresh and uplifting smell of citrus.
54. The relaxing aroma of a lavender hand cream or shower gel.
55. The joy of an old keepsake that evokes memories of happiness.
56. The peacefulness of lying down and watching clouds drift across the sky.
57. The relaxing feeling of brushing your hair or massaging your scalp.
58. The coziness of being wrapped in a warm blanket and wearing fuzzy socks.
59. The scrumptiousness of your favorite baked treat.

60. The gladness of discovering a little treasure in your favorite bookstore.
61. The serenity of watching the sunrise illuminate the darkness of night in the morning.
62. The feeling of contentment after a day spent outdoors in nature.
63. The excitement of a special occasion or upcoming holiday.
64. The satisfaction of having a good stretch after a long day.
65. The pleasure of gathering and organizing your thoughts in a journal.
66. Being enchanted by a delicious aroma or a nice, comforting fragrance.
67. The satisfaction of eating a wholesome, homemade meal.
68. The contentment of hearing the laughter of family and friends.
69. The enjoyment of creating something with your hands, whether cooking, baking, or crafting.

70. The calmness you feel after a moment of mindfulness.
71. The freedom to enjoy your evening as you like.
72. The gratefulness of seeing beauty around you.
73. The pleasure of stopping to smell the roses, figuratively and literally.
74. The luxury of a quiet, slow morning, with nothing on the calendar.
75. The tranquility of relaxing with a warm cup of tea in your favorite spot after a long day.

There is power in the little things—the power to comfort, the power to heal, and the power to make life beautiful. One might well consider the humble pleasures we tend to overlook to be the true source of joy in our days. And so, let us cherish the sweetness of the ordinary, for it is in the little things that happiness often dwells.

3

Tea Time: A Romance to Boost Joy Every Day

It is a mindset deeply admired and embraced: a heart in search of peace must first be willing to make a cup of tea and savor a quiet moment of simplicity. I eagerly await 4:00 PM, as this is the hour that changed everything for me. I open the small white cabinet at the bottom of my bookshelf, and I gingerly pull out my favorite tea set. This was my first porcelain tea set, gifted to me by my husband when we were best friends. Heart-shaped cups in pastel shades of pink, blue, yellow, green, orange, and burgundy elegantly sit atop matching saucers. This wasn't just a present that I had received for my birthday; it was the beginning of a new lifestyle.

In the midst of this new way of living, through the changing seasons and each passing afternoon, I look forward to my gentle routine with tea, calmness, and gratitude. I select a teapot—depending on how I feel, it might be a cheerful yellow teapot, a petite pink one, or my favorite, the one adorned with illustrations of fine chocolates. I put the kettle on and make an uplifting cup of Assam black tea; its robust aroma rejuvenates me with just one whiff. I pour the tea into my lovely pink tea cup, holding the gilded handle gently.

After adding a splash of milk and a teaspoon of sugar, I carefully stir with a little heart-shaped spoon. Being the scone enthusiast that I am, I often treat myself to freshly baked scones during afternoon tea. Regrettably, if I don't have warm scones in the kitchen, I'll look for a savory snack, a petite confection, or anything yummy that becomes even more delicious when dipped in tea.

I choose to enjoy my tea in my own company, seated on my favorite chair by the window, watching the rain-kissed garden outside. Technology is not permitted during this special time. This hour—still and silent—is reserved for deeply nourishing my mind, heart, and soul. I dedicate this time to noticing the beauty around me. I thoroughly immerse myself in each moment by paying attention to what I see, hear, smell, touch, taste, and how I feel. With appreciation, I acknowledge all the lovely little elements that embellish this moment. I surrender my heart to the present, encouraging myself to fully experience each and every sensation—the aromas, the textures, the tastes, the sights, and the sounds.

I open my gratitude journal and reflect on the blessings that have graced my day—good experiences, comforts, small joys, and cup-of-tea moments. I write down three of them and quietly sit with my thoughts of appreciation as I sip tea and savor this delightful time of the day. This joyful practice becomes my tiny daily habit of tea, gratitude, and beauty, and it changes everything.

After a long day, a few moments spent in the embrace of the present with a cup of tea, a sweet contentment settles upon me, lightening my heart's loads and filling my soul with peace. I start incorporating tea time into my routine for days, months, and years to come. Slowly, it becomes the daily hour that transforms, helping my body relax and simply be. It is when my heart opens, fully admiring and appreciating the daily beauty in my life. My soul relishes contentment. There is a small shift toward optimism in my mind, and it is certainly noticeable in my lifestyle. I now spend an hour each day engrossed in peace and positivity. Over time, it all adds up.

This is how a cup of tea, a moment of stillness, and a simple practice brought me a life I love. As the years passed, life brought with it many changes. Yet one thing remained constant in my life—my time steeped in joy every afternoon. Whether my husband sits nearby or my little ones are playing rambunctiously, I sit silently and pause for this moment of calm as the world carries on.

——— ✦ ———

Tea, time, and transformation. It is amazing how just one hour a day can change everything—how you relax, what you think about, and the lens through which you view the world. In the haste of everyday life, tea is not merely a nourishing drink. A cup of tea is a warm and gentle embrace, a welcome refuge from the rush.

Tea warmly invites you to live a quiet tale of love, a secret romance with life that opens your heart to the beauty and enchantment that surrounds you. I hold the belief that there is peace in tea leaves. Whether green, black, white, or herbal, each cup is nature's gift of calm to you.

The contentment a cup promotes is not simply a result of a wholesome beverage, but rather, in the state of mind it creates and the gratitude it invites. As the kettle begins to hum and the steam begins to rise, something magical starts taking form—not just in the cup, but in the heart of the tea-taker.

"Tea. The sweetness of love. The fragrance of flowers. The comfort of a friend. The warmth of a hug. Such great delight gingerly poured from a single pink teapot."

✦✦✦

Would you like to know how a cup of tea a day can change your life forever? A small cup of tea has the power to comfort a weary soul, to warm an aching heart, to uplift the low-spirited. Tea time invites us to infuse our daily routine with the calm joy of the little things—gently inspiring us to shift our attention not toward the things we wish we had, but toward the beauty that always was.

It is an elixir that encourages us to slow down, be present, and recognize the positives in our life—with an appreciative embrace. Simply brewing tea and taking the time to enjoy a cup can be a profound way to nurture mindfulness and gratitude with every sip, for it teaches you that happiness does not always present itself in a grand gesture. Sometimes, it may be nestled between tea leaves aromatic with scents of Earl Grey and bergamot.

In a world where we often see what other people have and what we might obtain, we might think about what we don't have rather than the abundance in our life. It is easy to overlook the quiet blessings and the unpretentious joys that already enrich our lives. Let us embrace tea, gratitude, and the art of slowing down.

GRATITUDE IN EVERY SIP

Tea time can be your daily gratitude reverie—a special time for counting your blessings and fostering a love for that which is already present. It can be a special time when your troubles melt like sugar in warm tea, and where the clink of the spoon against porcelain utters: there is so much to be thankful for.

Whether you make time for a warm cup in the morning, an afternoon tea, or an evening brew, tea time affords us an opportunity to pause and reflect on the good things in life. This tiny habit of tea and joy can help you live with more beauty and gratitude every day. Pick a time to be steeped in joy, and find a cozy and pleasant place to sit. Any setting that is calm and agreeable to you will be perfect. It could be in your happy place, a cozy corner of your home, or outside in nature, where you can refresh your mood and lift your spirits.

You might enjoy a robust blend, a comforting chai, a soothing chamomile, or even decaffeinated tea. As you sip your tea of choice, think about one thing you are grateful for with every sip you take. When you take your tea, remind yourself that even on the toughest of days, there is always a blessing that continues to blossom. It could be that very cup of tea, and quiet moment you have the pleasure of enjoying.

Choose your tea with intention. A tea blend that evokes positive feelings or a wonderful memory can help inspire gratitude. A calming tisane may welcome mindfulness. Tea, when sipped slowly and attentively, can inspire feelings of cozy contentment. As you relax, you can achieve a more positive, grateful mindset. Like a blooming flower, your heart opens to notice the beauty and embrace the joy already present in your everyday life.

Happiness asks us to love and care for ourselves, and happily, tea time is a deliberate act of self-care. Given the constant demands of daily life, it is essential to weave small acts of gentleness into your daily routine. Having a tea break or leisurely afternoon tea time is a special daily reminder to care for yourself. It's a chance to pause, put everything on hold, and take a moment to be kind to yourself. A pleasant experience you can look forward to every day, this meaningful tea time is a tender promise to dedicate moments of the day to nourishing and uplifting yourself.

Having a cup of tea in solitude also gives you a chance to fall in love with yourself. It empowers you to get comfortable with your own company, sitting with only your thoughts and feelings, and listening only to the whispers of your own heart.

You may like to adorn the hour with soft music or delicate fairy lights. Or, perhaps you are craving a special treat. As a declaration of self-love, tea time allows you to give yourself the same thoughtfulness you might offer a loved one.

Pour a cup full of love and compassion into your own heart and soul, for you are worthy of the gentlest care. Let tea time be your tale of tea, love, and gratitude—a quiet romance with your own heart and with the world around you. For with every cup of tea you pour, you have the chance to love a little deeper—both yourself and the little things in life. The simple act of using tea time to increase moments of beauty and joy can slowly shift your focus away from negativity, haste, and stress. Cherish this small comfort, as it can help invite more positivity, relaxation, and peace to your day.

A CUP OF MINDFUL CALM

Let us fall deeply in love with this moment, fully present in mind, body, and soul, in the sweet embrace of mindfulness. Being mindful means immersing yourself in the present moment without making judgments. Tea time invites us to fill our daily routine with more calmness and intentional presence—shifting our attention to only the beauty that adorns the hour.

Listen to the soothing sound of water slowly pouring over the tea leaves, infusing gratitude in every drop. Breathe in the enchanting aroma of the brewed tea, a swirl of steam, perfumed with rose and cardamom curls upward like a secret whisper saying: you are enough. Watch the warm steam rising from the cup of tea, slowly drifting away like any tension you may be holding on to. Invite your taste buds to embark on a flavorful adventure with each sip, musing about the tea's journey to your cup.

Let the joy steep slowly. Let every cup of tea quietly celebrate the present and your love for this very moment of life. Tea time reminds us to bring intention and beauty into our everyday—rejoicing in the habits that facilitate the bloom of joy and connection. For every leaf steeped, bask in the beauty that fills the hour.

And, with every sip, you have the chance to hold joy that is in the moment before you. The soft rustle of a tea sachet can become the melody that soothes the soul after a long day. Every cup of tea infuses a feeling of peacefulness and contentment that lingers long after the last sip.

"Joy grows in the gentle habit of sipping tea. A quiet moment all to myself: the cozy embrace of a cup held close, the small act of pouring milk just so, and stirring in sugar gently. Outside, the world hurries with clamor and speed—but inside, it's calm. I'm alone, but I'm not lonely. The world feels far away, and close, all at once."

✦✦✦

> **SIP OF INSPIRATION**
>
> As you sip tea, think about the comfort it provides. What other small joys bring you warmth and ease? How can you enjoy them at tea time?

4

Joy as a Daily Practice

Earth is a crown that adorns the universe, and you are a beautiful jewel sparkling in the crown. Your radiance, your exquisiteness, and your allure are some of the properties that make you shine. Your heartwarming smile is one of the most beautiful things about you; you can bestow this gorgeous gift on someone to brighten their day. Your resplendent eyes have glorious depth; they effortlessly reveal the hidden feelings that reign over your heart. Your face glows like the moon on a midsummer's night and emits light upon those around you. You are worthy of love and joy.

Feel your heartbeat, focus on your breath. Your mind has the power to think beautiful thoughts; your heart is a gift that helps create beautiful emotions. Be grateful for your ability to move, for your senses, for your heart, and for your mind. Appreciate the capabilities, the strength, and the resilience that your body provides you. Even in moments of vulnerability and imperfection, you are enough. Take care of your body, mind, and soul so that you may shine from within.

You give to others with a tender and caring heart, but what about the self? It gracefully carries you through each day with such strength and dedication. What do you do to ensure that it has the nourishment, rest, and care it needs to thrive on your journey? You deserve the same thoughtfulness and compassion that you extend to others. Whether you need nourishment, a little break from daily demands, or gentle words, self-care invites you to tune into your thoughts, feelings, wishes, and needs. Take time to listen to your body, to your mind, and to your heart. Respond to it with tender care.

HONOR YOUR BODY

As the vessel that carries you through this world, your body is most deserving of your deepest love and respect. Listen to its gentle whispers—its need for food, for rest, for fresh air and movement. Every day is a chance to meet oneself with kindness and care, though what that looks like can differ for each person. One might consider making time to eat a deliciously nutritious meal, enjoy a calm, quiet tea break, or go outside for a brisk walk. The first step in self-care is to attune yourself to your body, an essential part of the process.

Make self-care a daily practice, for nestled between moments of activity and rest, there are many quiet opportunities to engage in practices that nourish the self. You don't need to create a rigid self-care routine, but rather, to gently weave little habits of care that nurture you into your day. What you might need during a busy, demanding week may differ from what you usually need on a daily basis.

The preservation of the self may change with the seasons, when you may need to nourish your body and heart more deeply during cold winters. You might spend more time on creating moments of cozy comfort, sipping nourishing soups, and taking part in calming activities that bring little moments of happiness. There is something heartwarming about putting your fluffy socks on, wearing a favorite sweater, and reading a good book by the fire while sipping a cup of tea on a winter's night.

You may tend to yourself differently after the first bloom of spring. Fresh, vibrant, refreshing meals made with a bouquet of fruits and vegetables might be what the body craves. Joyful activities may take the form of a picnic or tea party with loved ones in the garden. You might like to enjoy a sweet ice cream treat during a lovely stroll on the beach or go for an invigorating jog in the sunshine.

You can enjoy many self-care practices all year long—the pleasure of a warm, aromatic bath to relax you after a long day, a gentle evening stretch, and simple deep breathing exercises. You might consider taking time to call a friend or a family member that you haven't had a chance to catch up with in a while. Think about creating a nourishing skincare routine for the season. Or, you might just like to spend a few quiet moments journaling to process your emotions. Listen to your body and, with intention, prioritize your own well-being by relishing small self-care practices that uplift you daily. Be good and gentle with yourself every day.

Nourish yourself with healthy food. Your body is a treasure box, safeguarding your precious assets—your mind, heart, and soul. In one way or another, it sends you a signal to let you know when the weather is gray and foggy inside. So that you may restore its brightness, nourish it with vibrant fruits and vegetables, giving it the strength that it needs to rise to the challenges of the day. Eat fresh, wholesome food that nurtures and supports your body from the inside out. A balanced diet rich in vitamins, minerals, and antioxidants can help support overall health. Remember to drink water, even if it means using a sticky note to remind yourself. Repeat after me: hydration is power. Use water and healthy food to express gratitude to the self, honoring the body that sustains your journey.

Eat something green. Or chocolate. Or both. On occasion, one must, without guilt, allow oneself the pleasure of indulging in a fine confection or a seriously scrumptious piece of cake. It can certainly be difficult to eat healthily all the time, given the constant temptation of delectable pastries and mouthwatering foods readily available. When you find yourself enthralled by the heavenly scent coming from the shiny chocolate bar, perhaps you might rip open the shiny wrapper, and devour it without guilt, as treating yourself from time to time is a splendid little way to find a glimmer of joy in the everyday.

Every night, promise yourself that you will take care of your body, and remind yourself to make good choices as soon as you wake up. Visit a dietitian and develop meal plans for yourself. Pick up a nutrition book and learn about how the foods you eat affect you today and tomorrow. Find a list of healthy foods and try to put together delicious recipes. Learn about healthy foods that can help release endorphins that uplift your mood.

Endorphins are the happy signals in the brain that are released by certain foods or experiences. You aim to feel energetic, healthy, and in good spirits. If your diet permits, you might consider incorporating foods that, according to science, can enhance your mood.

I may not be a healthcare professional, but I do know what healthy eating looks like. It is important to control both what you eat and how much you eat to maintain a healthy weight. Be mindful of your portion sizes. Eating from small plates and bowls is one simple trick that can be quite helpful. Mindless eating can lead to overeating. Practice mindful eating by taking your time to smell, taste, and experience the food.

Let the aromas captivate your senses and excite your taste buds. Let the variety of textures in your mouth hold your interest and inspire you to eat more slowly. Revel in the explosion of flavors and let it heighten the satisfaction you get from eating. As you relish each bite, think about where and how your food was grown, pondering its interesting journey to your table. You will enjoy your meal more and make it an experience.

It would be perfect if you could start your own little edible garden at home or a local community center; it's invigorating, compels you to eat healthier, and it's rewarding to eat what you grew with your own hands.

You can plant a fruit or vegetable of your choice. Herbs are wonderful, too. Perhaps you would like a garden blooming with basil, oregano, and mint, each vying with the others to be the healthiest and most fragrant gift to you.

You can decide whether to start with a seed or a flourishing plant. Place it directly in the soil or in a large pot you can keep in a convenient space, such as a patio or balcony. Care for your plants tenderly, and hopefully, one day, they will nourish you as well. Look forward to the day garden-fresh basil fills your home with a mouth-watering aroma and infuses your pasta with delicately sweet flavor.

Start each morning by giving yourself the gift of water to hydrate after a long night. A subtle yet essential act of self-care, drinking a glass of water first thing in the morning is like giving your body a gift for replenishment. Infuse a cup of water with fresh fruits or herbs to further elevate its goodness. Remember to pause briefly and breathe between each sip, slowly savoring each drop.

Make time for breakfast. Take a little time to lovingly prepare a light meal for yourself every morning. Simply slicing fruit can be relaxing and a mindful act. As you wash, cut, and arrange the fruits, pay attention to the sounds, colors, textures, and scents. As you make your tea, listen to the sound of the water boiling, smell the fragrance of the tea, and observe the steam rising in delicate curls. Turn the small, daily act of nourishment into a meditation, preferably sitting by a small window with sunlight streaming in to brighten your morning.

Having breakfast outside, in nature's embrace, can also help start the day with optimism. When you eat your food and drink your tea, do so slowly and attentively as you relish every bite and sip. Remind yourself that you are worthy of this effort, for it is a small act of kindness and gratitude toward your body, thanking it for supporting you on your journey.

Every day is a day to dress up for. Life is precious, and every day is worth celebrating, even if it means just putting on a nice outfit. Self-care includes dressing yourself well so that you can show up with confidence. Present your best self, even if you are just making a quick trip to the grocery store. Brush your hair and dress neatly so you can carry yourself gracefully wherever you choose to go. Dressing up and maintaining a tidy appearance are fun parts of self-care.

Prioritize physical activity. An essential part of preserving the self is making movement a daily self-care practice. Whether you choose a gentle or vigorous activity, it is important to move, stretch, and strengthen your body. Every day offers a new opportunity to honor your body through movement, whether you do a fun dance in your room, enjoy a brisk walk outside, have a leisurely yoga session, or play a quick game of tennis.

One may spend time playing with kids or pets. During a morning or afternoon stroll, try to take pleasure in the refreshing ambiance of local parks and gardens, boasting plush carpets and drapery of verdure. Whether you enjoy Zumba, Pilates, swimming, or sports, it can be helpful to engage your body in a physical activity you enjoy.

If time does not allow you to wander, you might focus on in-home activities that you can attempt in the comfort of your home. Play controller-free video games with your family to get some fun exercise right at home. One can find some space and do jumping jacks, jump rope, or jog in place. Gardening and yard work are also great ways to get fresh air and get your body moving.

Each day, you have the joy of choosing a form of movement that fits your schedule and mood. Simply taking a few moments to stretch can feel wonderful in the morning or after a long day. Every day you choose movement, you move closer to turning it into a valuable, tiny habit. Honor your body through physical activity, strengthening it so it is ready for a new day and all it brings. Movement and play can also lighten the mind and soul.

CALM YOUR MIND

Find peace in quiet pauses, in the spaces where silence lingers. Just as the body requires nourishment and movement, the mind, too, needs gentle nurturing. Consistently finding minutes of rest and peacefulness are essential to self-care.

As we meet the demands of daily life, it is ever important to remember to pause and just to be. This is a simple form of mindfulness. Be more present with your surroundings, with your thoughts, with the quietness. Consider quiet meditation, focusing on your breath in the stillness. Journaling can calm your mind, enabling you to release your thoughts and feelings on paper. The practice of reflecting through writing can help you let go, creating space in your mind for peace.

In the midst of daily obligations, it can be easy to forget one's own needs for replenishment. However, on busy days, when you are focused on your responsibilities, the need for self-care becomes especially essential. Every day, set aside time for a midday break to pause, rest, and reconnect with yourself.

A respite in the middle of the day, however brief, offers a chance to restore balance. Let us not spend this time staring at a screen or scrolling on our phone, but rather, doing something that truly benefits our well-being. This can look different for everyone, but the goal is to allow yourself to be fully present and embrace self-care. Perhaps you only have a few minutes to close your eyes and practice deep breathing. Taking a quiet moment to eat a meal, getting fresh air during a quick walk, and reading a few pages of a good book can help you rest and recharge.

A tea break is another enchanting daily act of self-care. If you are at work, at home, or somewhere else, a moment of pause can include a warm infusion in a peaceful corner or in nature. Relish the quiet moment by focusing on your tea, observing your surroundings, and letting yourself feel the sensations. This calm practice can be restorative for the body, mind, and soul.

BRIGHTEN YOUR SOUL

Nurture the soul with joy. Every single day of life, however busy and tiring it may be, is a gift. Each moment is precious and deserves to be respected and cherished. Between fulfilling your obligations and caring for yourself, create moments of joy by doing things that lift your spirits. Perhaps it is the feeling of the sunshine on your skin and the fresh air caressing you as you stroll outside, or the melody of a loved one lost in laughter.

Allow yourself to thoroughly enjoy these small moments. Seek out the tiny, bright moments of beauty that softly exist all around you. The sunlight streaming through the window, the flowers dancing in the garden, and the stillness of the world in the early morning are all opportunities to revel in the small wonders of life.

Joy, in all its beauty and complexity, can be found in the simple act of play. It can take the form of a spontaneous dance to your favorite song, a game with a friend, or laughter with a loved one. It can even be time spent painting or enjoying a creative activity. There are numerous ways to make play, laughter, and joy a part of your everyday life, allowing these blessings to seep into your soul and nourish you.

Some days, self-care may include comforting the soul by reaching out to a friend, spending quality time with family, and indulging in moments of laughter and shared experiences. You might like to spend time with those who make you happy. Surround yourself with good people who love you and support you.

Build quiet boundaries. Spend your energy with intention. Protecting your energy is an essential part of caring for yourself. Instead of committing to everything the world asks of you, save time for yourself and create space. Without guilt or shame, stand firm in your boundaries by saying *no* to things that you truly don't have the time or energy for. Determine if a demand or obligation truly needs to be met, and if so, by when. Try to avoid overburdening yourself or overcommitting. It is important to listen to your body and honor its needs.

Think about how you share your time and your presence, ensuring that you have plenty for yourself. To give to others, it is important first to replenish the self. Give yourself time and space to rest and restore your well-being. Self-care is essential to staying balanced, so you have the love and energy you need to give to yourself and others.

Ease into the evening. Develop tender habits that foster a graceful transition to the night. Create a space where you can step away from the day's demands and relax before you sleep. A calmer and more welcoming environment with dim lights, less noise, and soothing sounds can soften the evening. The relaxing scent of lavender or chamomile can evoke feelings of calmness. Whether you enjoy an aromatic bath, take a refreshing shower, or massage yourself with a rich cream or oil, it is important to have a tactile reminder that the body deserves love and care after a long day.

You might want to consider pampering yourself with aromatherapy. If you are not allergic or sensitive to fragrances, it can be nice to incorporate mood-boosting scents into your evening routine. Perfuming the air with uplifting scents can be a delicate way to impact emotions and well-being positively. I find that lavender has a soothing and calming effect on me. Due to its relaxing effect, I like to add this lovely scent to my nighttime self-care routine with a hand cream, shower gel, or hair care product.

Many people enjoy using essential oils to relax. Whether it is the zesty aroma of lemon or the refreshing scent of orange, citrus scents always uplift my mood, too. With their bright, joyful, energizing properties, citrus-scented facial cleansers or body washes often find their way into my morning skincare routine. Pampering yourself with beneficial products can help you achieve your most loved, radiant skin with gentle, nourishing ingredients. It's a little reminder that your body is worthy of such gentle attention. It is a little reminder that your body is worthy of such gentle attention.

Aim to get plenty of sleep. Your body works hard and needs an opportunity to refresh. Give yourself time to rest, for sleep is an important time for promoting wellness, a time for rejuvenation. Perhaps you may have to create a soothing environment to encourage a more peaceful slumber. Climb into a bed beautifully made with soft, fresh linens. Adjust the lighting, and try to ensure that the temperature in the room is comfortable. A serene sound of a waterfall or a gentle rain can be enjoyed in the background.

When it comes to self-care, small habits can make a big difference in how you feel. You can care for yourself simply by giving your body the time and space to heal itself through peaceful rest. Sleep not only rejuvenates your body and mind, but it also supports your soul, allowing you to rest, to heal, and to dream.

When you cultivate a deep connection with yourself through self-care, you realize that everything you need to create the life you want is already within you. This empowers your true self to rise—confident, radiant, and fully aligned with your light. Loving and caring for yourself and prioritizing your needs open your heart to love others and embrace the beauty around you. Don't deny yourself the quiet you need. Even flowers rest.

5

A Morning Routine that Changes Everything

The world is utterly quiet. The sun will make its graceful arrival shortly, gently gilding the world before my eyes. As the radiance slowly pours through the windows, I begin my day with tea, love, and thoughts of gratitude. Mornings can be hectic and rather rushed, especially with little loves to care for. I like to wake up early to have some time to myself. I begin my morning with a warm, cozy cup of tea, filling my kitchen with an uplifting aroma and my heart with calm.

I enjoy sitting by myself and indulging my mind and heart in beautiful contemplations—for that is what tea can inspire. Good thoughts, gratitude, and hope that the day will go well—these help me start the day with a positive mindset and an agreeable spirit. It is quiet, peaceful, and inspiring. With a cup of tea in hand, I ask myself two questions. What is one thing you love about yourself? What are three things you are grateful for today? With positive energy to brighten my morning, I am ready to start the day.

I encourage my little ones to begin their morning with a bright outlook, too. As my daughter enjoys her breakfast, I ask her to answer these two questions every morning. What is one thing you love about yourself? Her reply is usually, "My heart." What is one thing you are grateful for today? Her reply is something like, "Freshly baked bread and hot chocolate," and my toddler replies, "Kitty cat!" joyfully mentioning a favorite stuffed toy. These are two important questions I ask my children every morning. This simple practice inspires us to focus on the good things we are blessed with and helps us start the day as a family with positivity.

———— ✦✦✦ ————

The tranquil twittering of birds wakes you up to the calming sight of your cozy haven. The cool breeze sneaks into your window, softly caresses your cheeks, and greets you, "good morning." The cushioned bed cradles you while the duvet embraces you with warmth.

Wake up with a grateful heart, knowing you get to live another day. This pleasant morning marks the fresh beginning of a wonderful day ahead of you. Are you among the people who meet the weekday sunrise with reluctance rather than readiness? Remember that every day of life is worthy of appreciation.

Build a life you love so that you may look forward to every day of it. Make your days a little more beautiful with habits of positivity, love, and gratitude. Intentionally create moments of beauty and happiness by indulging yourself in the lovely little things that life gifts you. Each day of the week can be rewarding in its own special way, and you can find a quiet spark of joy in every day.

Whether you like to wake up early or sleep in, try to set aside some time to prepare yourself for a good day. Make conscious choices to cultivate happiness in your day with simple yet impactful practices. A bright and enriching day often starts the moment you wake up. A well-crafted morning routine that includes a positive intention, gratitude, and affirmations can set the tone for your day.

START THE DAY WITH POSITIVITY

Whisper a kind promise to yourself as soon as the day begins. The moment you open your eyes, quietly lie in bed for a bit, and set a positive intention. Choose one that is short, sweet, and uplifting so that you can easily remember it. Please write it down in your planner or on a sticky note so that you can keep it close by.

> I will be kind to myself today.
> I will focus on my blessings.
> I will be patient.
> I will be present.
> I will make healthier food choices.
> I will take small breaks.

Through your actions, focus on nurturing this intention throughout the day and gently remind yourself when you forget.

SAY GOOD MORNING WITH GRATITUDE

As you take a shower or prepare breakfast, take a few deep breaths and think about three things you are grateful for right now. They don't have to be anything extraordinary; they can be simple things such as a good night's sleep, a new day and beginning, or the pleasure of having some time to start the day quietly. This grateful mindset can set a positive tone for your day. Aspire to shift your focus away from the tasks ahead of you today or the stresses and anxieties that might be troubling you.

Take this time to think about the warmth in the little things.

Starting each day with gratitude and consciously choosing to appreciate your simple pleasures is a gentle discipline. Train your mind to focus on the good things in your life, carrying this positivity with you throughout the day. Aim to embrace appreciation more fully by weaving simple gratitude exercises into your daily routine. In the afternoon, you could take a short pause to reflect and write down three things you're thankful for in your journal. This is a small yet mighty practice that can shift your mindset, nourish the spirit, and recenter your heart.

Consider adding powerful affirmations to your morning routine to start your day with bright, beautiful energy. Affirmations are positive statements that can help you uplift your mindset, reduce stress, and boost confidence. Repeating self-empowering statements regularly can help us rewire our minds. Listening to and reciting healing words can help our bodies release endorphins and serotonin, contributing to positive emotions and feelings of happiness. Feel free to recite these affirmations in your mind or out loud.

POSITIVE MORNING AFFIRMATIONS

- I am grateful for a new day.
- I open my heart to the present moment.
- I feel peaceful and light.
- I love and accept myself.
- My life is beautiful and meaningful.
- I am exactly where I'm meant to be.
- Today is a new adventure waiting to unfold.
- It's a new page in my storybook.
- Today is a chance to stop and smell the roses.
- I am ready to find beauty in the everyday.
- I am strong.
- I am confident.
- I have everything I need to succeed.
- I believe in myself.
- I nourish myself with joyful foods and kind words.
- I choose to see the beauty around me.
- I am capable of achieving my goals.

- I am worthy of love and respect.
- Everything is happening for my greatest good.
- I let go of negative thoughts and embrace positive ones.
- I deserve compassion, especially from myself.
- I am alive. I am blessed.
- I am grateful for the good things in life.
- I am enough, just as I am. I celebrate my unique qualities.
- I am ready to shine.
- I am ready to have a great day.
- Today, I choose joy.

It would be wonderful if you could repeat these feel-good phrases every day for twenty-one days as a part of your morning routine. This practice can transform the way you think and feel about things. It is my dearest wish that repeating these affirmations every morning may lift your spirits, transform your mindset, and change your life.

6

When Love Becomes a Daily Practice

In London, we arrive at the iconic hotel, glittering with unparalleled opulence and grandeur. With an air of extravagance, it exudes timeless elegance that mesmerizes me at once. This moment—the culmination of my afternoon tea experiences in England—is one I have been dreaming of for some time. I am ready to revel in a most scrumptious selection of cakes and confections. I am ready to celebrate the union of our love.

The soft hum of the pianist in the background sets the perfect mood for the dreamy evening. Chic and glamorous, I wear a beautiful pink coat adorned with golden buttons and ivory faux fur. My ears sparkle with glamourous bow-and-pearl earrings my other half gifted me earlier in the day. Strands of lustrous pearls drape from my neck. My husband, dressed smartly, is a creature of exquisite refinement. He carries with him a graceful strength, the kind born not of arrogance, but of an insightful soul well acquainted with calmness, thought, and restraint. He pours me a cup of Earl Grey in the daintiest of porcelain teacups, tastefully embellished with a delicate blue flower pattern. The steam rising in elegant curls fills the air with a most comforting aroma on the cold evening.

A waiter brings forth a three-tiered stand, laden with traditional finger sandwiches—cucumber, smoked salmon, and egg and cress—followed by warm scones served with clotted cream and strawberry jam, just as they should be. As a connoisseur of scones, my eyes brightly sparkle with joy as I take my first bite; it is light, buttery, and warm, as proper a scone as one could wish for. My face, radiant with elation, catches my husband's eye, and he smiles.

For dessert, they serve us the finest of cakes and pastries, all of which look too good to eat: chocolate éclairs, lemon tarts, and a rich chocolate raspberry cake that melts in my mouth. A trolley arrives, and on it are more delectable cakes to enjoy. Everything is positively divine. We devour the sweet and savory delicacies that grace the table, indulging in every bite, savoring every moment. As we cheerfully talk about happy things and laugh our hearts out, we experience the joy of connection that will warm our hearts for many years to come.

As the evening fades into night, the city's lights filter through the large windows, casting a glow over the room. We sip the last of our tea, both content and peaceful in each other's company. It isn't just the luxury afternoon tea that makes the experience spectacular. It is about the joy of being together in an exciting new place, sharing an enjoyable experience, and creating memories to celebrate our bond.

Joy doesn't exclusively grow in the grandeur of palaces or landmarks, but in the quiet, in-between spaces, too. It brews in a tearoom just off a rain-slicked street in London, where steam curls from a vintage cup and cheerful voices blend with the clink of silver spoons like a song that soothes the soul.

We leave happy—our bodies full of confections and our hearts brimming with contentment. As we walk away, my arm wrapped around his, the warmth of the evening lingers. I sit down with my best friend outside, watching the world rush past, while time seems to pause. It slows down enough for me to notice that I am—for this moment—content.

This experience, steeped in tea and love, is quite simply an unforgettable moment of connection. Yet, our other tea dates in small, quaint tea shops across England have been just as beautiful and memorable. You see, it's not just about how grand the experiences are or where they occur; it is about the love and the bond you and your companion have. It is about celebrating the beauty of your relationship and noticing the magic of the moment you share.

Whether it is your significant other, a friend, or a family member, afternoon tea can be a really fun way to connect over a meaningful experience. It's a gentle way to bond with someone, adding a little extra warmth and enchantment. A quaint little tea shop or café, a luxury hotel, and a beautiful park all make lovely settings for tea.

If possible, consider forgoing a few unnecessary purchases to save money for a better experience, because the relationships that enrich our lives are the most worthwhile investment. Oftentimes, it is the little adventures that bring great joy and unforgettable memories that will forever hold a special place in our hearts.

Take time to celebrate the valuable relations in your life—with your loved ones, your favorite family members, your best friend, for it is love, and celebration of that love, that fills life with beauty and laughter.

Loving oneself. The love you feel for family and friends. Your beloved. Love for nature, and love for all living things. Love, in all its beautiful forms, is powerful, and the relationships they enrich life with are priceless. A bejeweled emotion that is as pure as a blossoming flower, love is the most precious gift worthy of gratitude.

One should never take one's most dear relationships for granted. In our busy and often chaotic lives, we may at times forget that love cannot simply maintain itself without our time and effort. Whether it is love for yourself, family, your significant other, or friends, it asks for attention and intentional nurturing. Love is a daily practice that needs deliberate care to thrive and fill our lives with beauty and fragrance.

Weave small habits of love into your daily life to strengthen your connections, deepen your bonds, and maximize the love in your life. There are many modest yet deeply impactful ways to make everyday life sparkle by adorning it with adoration.

From the love we give ourselves to the bonds we share with others—familial, romantic, or platonic—each relationship needs to be cultivated to grow. The dear bond shared with a parent, the passionate connection with a romantic partner, and the deep trust between friends all require time and thoughtful attention.

CHERISHING YOURSELF

From a place of self-love, you practice nurturing inner compassion and become kinder to yourself. You speak to yourself with gentleness and empathy. Taking time to celebrate yourself regularly becomes important. Acknowledging your achievements starts to matter. Whether you achieve a goal, learn something new, or overcome a challenge, applaud every win, no matter how small. Every day, remind yourself that you are deserving of love and respect.

THE WARMTH OF FAMILY

To nurture love in the heart of your family, consider calling your parents more often or sending little messages of gratitude to remind them they are cherished. With time, attention, and warm words of appreciation, you can strengthen family ties. If you live close by, you might consider visiting regularly, running an errand to help out, or cooking a delicious meal for them. Small, thoughtful acts can help strengthen the foundation of love, which usually begins in the family.

Practice active listening to strengthen bonds. Whether it's your family, friends, or partner, make a conscious effort to truly listen to what they say. Instead of waiting for your turn to speak or quickly jumping in to offer your opinion, patiently hear them out. Engage with what they are saying. Actively listening, showing empathy, and validating their feelings is a form of love and honoring them. This simple act can help you deepen your understanding of those who are closest to your heart.

A LOVE THAT BLOSSOMS

A romantic relationship might need small loving gestures every day. Express love daily through thoughtful little acts that remind your partner that you treasure them. Consistency is key. You might leave sweet notes for your partner to find, plan little surprises, or regularly have mini adventures to keep your love blooming and exciting. Pay attention when your partner is speaking, listening actively so that they know they are important to you.

Remember to praise your partner's accomplishments, skills, and talents so they feel appreciated and adored. Remember never to put them down, because they may be counting on you to lift their spirit. Shower your partner with words of warmth, affection, and encouragement to show you admire them.

KINDRED SPIRITS

In your friendships, being there and present is a nice way to show you care. Genuinely express interest in the lives of your favorite people. Whether it is with a compliment or beautiful flowers, celebrate the joys and successes of your friends by truly being happy for them. Offer support when they need it most. You could send a thoughtful text message, bake them a treat, help with a project, or quickly catch up over tea or coffee. Should the opportunity arise, you can invite your friend or a few friends over for an agreeable afternoon tea where you can talk and have a pleasant time, at your leisure.

Nurture love daily, turning it into a beautiful tiny habit that can boost the sense of contentment you experience each day. Reflect on small steps you can take to prioritize acts of fondness within your schedule. There are many excellent practices you can incorporate into your daily routine to keep love blossoming.

Start each day with gratitude and carry a mindset of love and abundance throughout the day. Take time to think about the people you adore and the joy they bring to your life. Ask yourself who the most important people in your life are. What do you truly appreciate about each person, and when was the last time you shared this with them? How much presence and attention do you offer to those you care about? Thoughtful little gestures can remind your favorite people that they are loved and treasured.

Prioritize small acts of kindness and affection, for sometimes, love doesn't have to be expressed verbally. It can just be felt in the thoughtfulness behind the little things we do each day. Send a caring text to check in on a friend. Leave a heartfelt note for your partner. Lovingly make a card or a craft and give it to a person you care about. Bake cookies and make someone's day a little sweeter. Take a friend out for a treat or meal to show that you value them.

Whether you gift kind words, thoughtful acts, or memorable moments, cherishing love with kindness can give back. Your family may become closer to you and more engaged in your life. Your friends might become more open with you, deepening the trust you share. Your partner may become more affectionate, allowing love to bloom more fully.

One of the most beautiful truths is that love isn't limited to your closest relationships. Once you turn love into a daily habit, you may become more attuned to the world around you. A kind word to someone who needs a little sunshine, a simple act to lift someone's spirits—love can also be generous in charitable ways. Perhaps you might leave out water for cats in your neighborhood on a hot day. Plant flowers, trees, or a vegetable garden to lovingly nurture nature. Respect the earth by treating it with care. Every act of kindness done out of love will bring to you, in return, love.

Love is like a rose, and, the more we cherish it, the more beautiful it grows. And in doing so, you may hopefully find yourself surrounded by an abundance of meaningful, fulfilling relationships that fill your heart with joy. Love, when nurtured and practiced, has the power to shift our mindset toward abundance and joy.

It's not a fleeting feeling. It's not an occasional emotion. Love is a lifestyle, requiring intentional practice that is woven into your everyday routine. A life full of love and compassion is one with stronger relationships, increased joy, deeper connections, and greater meaning. Choose love, whether it is through small acts of kindness, meaningful conversations, or quaint tea parties melodious with the laughter of loved ones. For ultimately, love is the energy that breathes magic and life into our world.

7

Tea, Scones, and the Joy of Being Together

I have long been captivated by the cozy charm of tea shops and tearooms, picturesque havens where the air is rich with a welcoming warmth. Through the doors we find the promise of a lovely cup of tea, offering with it moments of beauty and quiet joy. Back when I was in college, I came really close to realizing this dream of opening up my very own fanciful little tearoom.

It would be a tranquil sanctuary where guests could escape the clamor of the day, unwind with an aromatic pot of tea, and eat scrumptious scones lovingly baked from recipes passed down to me from my mother. It would be a lighthearted place where one could come to enjoy gentle company, laugh, and enjoy an afternoon of quiet indulgences, from petite sandwiches to dainty cakes. I envisioned that it would be a special space for celebrating life, ourselves, and our dearest relationships.

Yet, the combination of my studies and other projects led me to follow a different direction. Still, in the quiet corners of my heart, the reverie of such a place remained a sweet dream that I cherished.

Although this aspiration had not been fully realized, the past decade led me on an interesting journey during which I planted the seeds for a similarly beautiful blossom. My home, prettily presented as a charming tearoom, is now a refuge of warmth and enjoyment for my family. The air is fragrant with the soothing scent of lavender tea, the sweet and uplifting notes of a chocolate and rose blend, and the comforting spice of chai. And though I do not get to pour tea for guests like I once envisioned, I still share this joy, mailing my teas to distant souls, spreading a little comfort and happiness wherever they may be.

Adorned with fresh flowers, romantic décor, and inspirational quotes, my bookshelf is also a whimsical reflection of my dream. It is brimming with uplifting books and gratitude journals whose pages I've poured my most beloved thoughts into. Through my online store, I send off these tender treasures to people everywhere—brightening their day and inspiring them to savor quiet moments of beauty daily through gentle habits of tea and joy.

With every order of loose-leaf tea and books that I affectionately pack for shipment, I aspire to inspire people everywhere to bask in the enchantment of my tea-scented, flower-filled, rose-colored haven. Although they cannot sit beside me in person, they, too, can revel in the warmth and joy of it all from their own cozy corners. That, in itself, fills my heart with the deepest gratitude and joy.

Let us beautify everyday life with the romance of tea time. Let every cup of tea be an invitation to fall in love—with the hour, the stillness, the heart that beats within, and the beauty that blossoms before you.

―― ✦ ――

Build authentic bonds with tea. On my journey of cultivating love as a daily practice, I gladly developed a habit of celebrating and strengthening heartfelt relationships over a cup of tea.

Tea is more than just a drink; it's an opportunity to pause, embrace gratitude, and share love with others. The daily act of brewing a cup of tea becomes my quiet time to reflect on my relationships and to show gratitude to the people who fill my life with joy.

Enjoy a cup of tea with a friend, family member, or coworker to deepen bonds. Nurture love over tea with your beloved. Share a cup (or two) with a special person whose laughter makes each sip sweeter. Socializing and connecting with others over a cup of tea, an offering of kindness and warmth, can be a gentle and meaningful way to nourish our souls together.

When seeking ways to make life more fulfilling and joyful, cultivating positive, supportive relationships can be essential. Sipping tea together is a lighthearted indulgence you can delight in to connect with someone while having a nourishing drink, engaging in a relaxing conversation, laughing, and being present. Often found in the little moments of everyday life, happiness can be *shared* by curling up with tea and good company.

I love hosting tea parties—gathering around the table, sipping from delicate teacups, and getting lost in the warmth of togetherness. These fun gatherings are not just about the tea itself, but rather, about appreciating each other's presence, actively listening, and engaging in joyful conversations.

Whether it's a casual afternoon with a loved one or a more elaborate celebration, tea parties have become my way of fostering love and cherishing my relationships. I also use my much-loved scones to sweeten my bonds, baking a tray to take to the family I will be visiting for tea.

The act of serving tea feels symbolic—each cup I pour represents my love and appreciation for the person sitting across from me. I take time to prepare my space with care, ornamenting the table with beautiful flowers, lovingly arranging homemade goodies, selecting uplifting tea blends, and creating an atmosphere of beauty and warmth. Family and friends are often smitten with the thoughtful details, appreciating that I put in time and effort into doing something special for them. My tea parties—whimsical with bunting and mismatched tea sets—become a special occasion where love is celebrated, laughter is shared, and bonds are strengthened.

Through my love of tea, I come to understand the importance of creating space for connection in my life. It's not just about the tea; it's about the intention behind it. The time I spend with others—focused and present—is a gift of love that fosters deeper relationships and helps create the utterly bewitching moments that brighten up life.

Tea, sugar, and smiles: this may be the recipe for joyful connection. When the moment allows, think about ways you can celebrate love with tea to warm hearts, soothe souls, and lift spirits.

HOW TO ENJOY A DAY STEEPED IN TEA & LOVE

☕ Morning tea and self-love.
Start your morning with a warm cup of tea to nourish and uplift yourself. Repeat positive affirmations such as, "I am worthy of love and respect."

♥ Tea date.
Whether it's at a tea shop or in a cozy setting at home, have regular tea dates with your partner. Be present to fully enjoy a peaceful moment of connection, listening actively, and engaging thoughtfully.

☕ Afternoon tea.
Invite family, a friend, or your partner. Reserve a table at a tea room or prepare afternoon tea at home. Select an aromatic tea and treats. Share uplifting words and happy moments. What a wonderful way to sweeten the hour with sweets, laughter, and the magic of friendship.

♥ Monthly tea parties.
Prioritize gatherings that bring people together over tea, treats, and moments of warmth. Whether it is once a month or on holidays, having tea parties means bringing

all of your favorite people together to nourish love and nurture relationships with delicious food and laughter.

☕ Tea and a favorite pastime.
Choose a person to enjoy tea and a hobby with regularly. If you and your companion enjoy reading, perhaps you may like to have a book club, enabling you to read and discuss good books over a cup of tea. If you enjoy nature, you may like to go for a walk and pour a cup of tea from a thermos to enjoy at the park.

♥ Tea adventure with partner.
Love can take you places to which there were previously no routes. Plan a romantic getaway with your beloved, and surely, you may find a tender moment to cherish your love over a cup of tea. Take a trip to a charming town with an oceanfront where you two can dine and spend quality time together, sipping tea along the way.

Walk to the beach hand-in-hand. Fondly hold each other while you watch the sublime, saffron sunset together in wonderment—marvel at the gloriousness of the setting sun. The love you share is also exquisite. The infinite water is unchangeable and everlasting. Your love can also be this way.

☕ Tea in the night.

Elope for a dreamy adventure in the secrecy of the night. Take a blanket, fill a thermos with warm tea, and go on a long drive. Find a romantic setting—a spot that has breathtaking views with which you will both become enamored.

Cuddle up in the car or on a bench outside, and gaze at the twinkling stars. Focus on only this moment and only this person, forgetting about everything else in the world. The crickets chirp, the wind rustles, and trees dance gracefully. With stardust in your eyes, nestle your head on your beloved's shoulder, and listen to nature compose the music of the night.

> "Few afternoons are as agreeable as afternoons aromatic with uplifting tea, sweetened with confections, melodious with the laughter of a loved one."

✦✦✦

Keep tea and love flowing in your relationships. There is much contentment and joy in the simple act of sharing a cup of tea with loved ones. Tea has the power to nourish love, deepen bonds, and bring joy to us all.

Moments that are cordially infused with tea bring people together to nurture connection, laughter, and joy, so keep sharing love through a full pot.

> **SIP OF INSPIRATION**
>
> What ideas do you have for enjoying a day steeped in tea and love? Do you think you can make time for any of these once a month?

8

Embrace the Sunset: A Calm Evening Routine

As the sun dips below the horizon, it's time to ease into a well-crafted evening routine that sets the stage for restful sleep, personal reflection, and emotional well-being. While the amount of free time you have will determine your evening, the goal is to enjoy meaningful little practices that bring you peace and contentment.

Let yourself be immersed in the serenity of the evening. This special time is a gift—an opportunity to ease into a state of relaxation, reflect on the good things that happened during the day, and take care of yourself. After a long and busy day, it's easy to feel drained and overwhelmed. But with a more lighthearted approach, the evening can become an experience of peace and cozy contentment. A good evening routine doesn't just help you wind down physically; it also nurtures your mental and emotional state. It's a time to focus on rest, prioritize self-care, and enjoy an uplifting activity, all of which contribute to an unspoken gladness.

Disconnect from the chaos. One of the first steps to creating a peaceful evening is to disconnect from the outside world. As the day ends, it's time to step away from the stress and demands of technology. By limiting screen time—especially social media and work emails—you free yourself from tension and distractions, creating space for relaxation. Consider putting away your devices or setting a time when you stop responding to work messages. This small act of digital detox gives your mind permission to slow down and embrace a more serene evening. Welcome the gentle fade of day, relishing the peacefulness of the evening.

Create moments of joy with simple acts. A cozy evening routine—one that calms and uplifts—is created by small yet intentional moments that bring peace and enjoyment. It could include a small but soothing ritual such as lighting a candle, putting on a pair of fluffy socks, sipping a cup of herbal tea, or eating something healthy and delicious. The little things not only soothe the senses but can also help signal to your brain that the day is ending. Putting on your favorite pajamas and a pair of cozy socks, or curling up with a warm blanket, can transform your space into a comfy haven where you can fully relax and be present in the moment.

EVENING ROUTINE FOR A HAPPIER TOMORROW

Unwind with a relaxing activity. A joyful evening routine may also include an activity that brings your soul contentment. It could be reading a good book, listening to a soothing podcast, practicing mindfulness, writing in your gratitude journal, or spending time on a creative hobby. Engaging in these enjoyable activities allows you to disconnect from the demands of the day and connect to something that makes you feel good. Whether it's immersing yourself in the pages of a nice novel, painting, writing, or knitting, creative pursuits can help shift your focus away from routine obligations and fill your evening with a bit of joy. Spend a while wrapped up in an activity that feels relaxing and comforting.

Engage in self-nurturing. Remember to make time for self-care, as it can be beneficial for both your body and mind. A deeply comforting aromatic soak, a pampering skincare routine, gentle stretches, and deep breathing are a few options. Caring for your physical body can help release tension, alleviate stress, and prepare you for restful sleep. Taking time to nourish your skin or practice mindfulness gives you a moment of calm, love, and appreciation for yourself. These kind practices are a reminder that you deserve to feel good, both inside and out, before you end your day.

Design a tranquil bedtime environment. The atmosphere you create as you prepare for bed can significantly influence how restful your sleep is. A cozy, serene setting signals to your body that it's time to rest. You could begin by dimming the lights and ensuring the bedroom is quiet and composed for the evening.

A calming scent from essential oils like lavender or chamomile can perfume the air with tranquility. A thoughtfully dressed bed, adorned with plump pillows and a lovely blanket, offers a most inviting place to rest. You might want to adjust the temperature to a level conducive to sleep. The more comfortable and serene your space, the easier it will be to let go of the day and drift into restful slumber.

Think about the good things. As night falls, take a moment to reflect on the positive aspects of your day. What simple pleasure did you enjoy today? Did you get a chance to connect with a loved one? Was there a moment that filled you with a sense of contentment?

Maybe you indulged in a decadent treat, spent time in nature, had a nice chat with a friend, or completed an important task. Ending your day with gratitude can help you fall asleep feeling a bit calmer and more at peace. It's good to go to bed with a reminder that much beauty and joy exist in your life.

Gratitude has the power to shift our perspective, gently guiding our focus away from stress and challenges toward the blessings in our lives. This wonderful practice can help nurture a positive mindset and foster a sense of contentment as you ease into sleep. Taking this opportunity to reflect on what went well during your day and honor your growth can ease your mind and create space to release lingering worries.

As you settle into bed, think about a positive intention you would like to set for the next day. This could be something simple, such as speaking to yourself with kind words, practicing mindful eating, or pausing to notice the beauty around you. Setting a small, hopeful goal for the following day can ignite a feeling of purpose and motivation, giving you something to look forward to as you drift off to sleep. It's a practice that can encourage an optimistic mindset and set the tone for the next day.

A thoughtful routine encourages you to slow down and appreciate the quiet moments, especially after the day has asked so much of you. When you intentionally create a joyful nighttime routine, it has a ripple effect, bringing a ray of positivity to your life. The peaceful energy you cultivate at night can carry over into the next day, like a ray of sunshine to brighten up your morning. You may wake up feeling more rested and content, mentally clearer, and emotionally grounded. Set yourself up for a brighter, more joyful tomorrow.

Joy often grows in small habits that might be easily overlooked: opening windows to let in the cold breeze at the end of the day, folding laundry still warm from the dryer, lighting a candle to soften the evening. When you pause briefly to notice, you'll see that there are many quiet delights to be enjoyed at the day's end.

> **SIP OF INSPIRATION**
> Create your own cozy evening routine. Brew a warm drink, wrap yourself in a blanket, and let go. What is it that brings you calm as the day draws to a close?

9

The Cup That Powers Habit

The steam rises gracefully from my morning cup of tea, carrying an enlivening scent of spiced chai into the quiet kitchen. As thoughts about the tasks ahead of me pour in, I am mentally prepared to rush through this cup that is meant to infuse my soul with cozy comfort. As a busy creative and mom of two, my mornings feel like a race against the clock. Between breakfast, lunches, emails, and school drop-offs, there's a whirl of things to do that leave me breathless before the day even begins. I hadn't realized how often rushing had become my default, shaping my mindset before I even had a chance to choose.

After recognizing that a special time of day is not being optimized for wellness and joy, I decided to start dedicating my first cup of tea to alignment instead of acceleration. Rather than gulping my tea without even thinking, I begin engaging with my daily brew as a gentle five-step ritual that grounds me before the day pulls me in.

Each morning, I take a moment to intentionally *select* my tea based on my mood or the feeling I want to cultivate. Sometimes it's a bright, floral herbal blend for motivation. Other days, I choose something robust and supportive. This simple act of choosing becomes my *cue*—the shift from chaos to clarity, and the transition from rushing to stepping into presence.

While my tea *steeps*, I ask myself a thoughtful question: "What matters most for me to show up well today?" A single word, such as patience, focus, or preparation, carries my intention. With the first *sip* I take, I embrace the moment, allowing my senses to center and calm me. As I continue sipping, I choose one tiny action connected to my intention—something small enough to complete even on the busiest mornings. I then *savor* this micro-action, whether it's a deep breath, a choice, or a brief two-minute review of my schedule. Though these are little practices, they make my intention tangible.

Before finishing my cup, I either *write down* my intention in a journal or *share* it with someone close to me. This step reinforces the identity I'm nurturing: "I am someone who begins each day with clarity, purpose, and presence." Writing my words makes it feel more real. It becomes a tangible reminder I can return to when the day feels messy. During this process, I learned that my days can begin with intention, and sometimes, that's all it takes to change everything.

Within weeks, this soothing ritual, which I call the Teatimely Habits Method, transforms my mornings. It turns my tea into more than a quick morning drink—it becomes an important moment of alignment. Unlike my afternoon tea—which reliably offers a moment of calm, mindfulness, and infuses the hour with gratitude and beauty—my morning cup becomes the one that powers habit.

Of course, the whirlwind doesn't disappear. Kids still need breakfast, emails drift in steadily, but *I* change. My clarity grows. My inner pace shifts. The first cup of the day starts to feel like a guiding light, illuminating the path toward the kind of day that I want to create. Each morning starts to feel less like a rush and more like a grounding—a gentle beginning, a conscious choice.

The Teatimely Habits Method is a unique and distinctly delightful habit-building framework that anchors intentional behavior to a stable daily *cue*—tea time. It softly guides us through a beautifully structured sequence of micro-choices, sensory engagement, reflection, and identity reinforcement. By combining a built-in cue (teatime), a simple moment of selection, a calming sensory *routine* (Steep → Sip → Savor), a brief sharing or recording, and an intrinsic *reward* loop of Calm → Clarity → Identity, this method creates a supportive habit rhythm. Grounded in research-informed behavioral principles, it helps habits become easier to start, repeat, and integrate into who you are.

HOW HABITS FIND THEIR WAY

At its heart, every habit follows a simple pattern. Something nudges you to begin, you move into the behavior, and your brain feels a small but significant sense of satisfaction. Repeat that rhythm often enough, and it begins to flow naturally.

Journalist Charles Duhigg popularized this idea through what he calls the "Habit Loop": a cue that sparks the behavior, a routine that carries you through it, and a reward that makes you want to repeat it. While many researchers have expanded this concept in various ways, the core truth is straightforward—habits become automatic when a consistent trigger leads to an action that feels good and is repeated until effortless.

What tends to be missing, though, is a habit loop that truly feels comforting, gentle, and easy to return to—especially on busy or emotionally challenging days. People don't merely struggle with habits because they don't understand the cue–routine–reward model. The real challenge lies in discovering a habit loop that feels soft, sustainable, and easy to embrace, even on tough days.

This is where the tea ritual becomes so powerful. A cup of tea naturally contains everything the habit loop requires: a built-in cue, a calming routine, a heartening reward, and a moment that deepens your connection to who you are. It turns habit-building into something soft, sensory, and balanced—something your mind and body actually look forward to.

In this book, we use the well-known Habit Loop as a foundation, and we use teatime—a familiar and comforting daily moment—as a powerful habit anchor. When you pair a new behavior with something that you already do consistently, such as steeping or sipping your tea, the brain embraces the new habit with greater ease. Teatime becomes the built-in cue: a gentle whisper that it's time to step into your chosen action. The soothing ritual of tea also provides an immediate sense of calm and clarity, making the entire habit feel natural, enjoyable, and sustainable.

THE TEATIMELY HABITS METHOD

My 5-step Teatimely Habits Method is not a new habit loop; it is a ritual framework that sits inside the loop, making each stage more intentional, mindful, and meaningful. Teatime is predictable, sensory, soothing, invites reflection, and it's already a habit for many people. In addition, the ritual environment reduces friction. It all makes tea time an ideal anchor for habit formation.

The tea ritual doesn't replace the habit loop—it simply gives your brain a beautiful, structured way to move through it. Select, Steep, Sip, Savor, and Share guide you through setting an intention, engaging your senses, choosing a small action, and reinforcing your identity. The tea ritual enhances the cue, enriches the action, and makes the reward deeply felt.

Teatimely Framework
Select → Steep → Sip → Savor → Share

WHY THIS FRAMEWORK NURTURES ANY HABIT

This special, tea-based framework is not just about tea—tea simply serves as an *anchor*, allowing a wide variety of habits to flourish. Some of the main categories include mindfulness and presence, reflection and journaling, identity-building, slow-productivity and creativity, emotional regulation, connection and relationships, self-care and well-being, and more.

Many of the habits that we journey through together in this book can also be nurtured through the Teatimely Habits Method. This agreeable approach provides a sensory-rich way to add positive routines to your daily life, turning small actions into meaningful experiences. However, exploring each habit in depth would be beyond the scope of this gentle guide. My intention here is to offer inspiration and support, giving you the tools to weave these habits into your life at your own pace. Some habits may come naturally while others may take time to settle in—and that's entirely natural. You might enjoy exploring one of them through my habit-building framework, or you may follow your intuition and try nurturing the habit in your own way—both paths are perfectly okay. This journey is about finding joy and presence in your everyday life, in ways that feel authentic and nourishing to you.

THE QUIET POWER OF THE TEATIMELY METHOD

This simple tea ritual is more than just a cup of tea—it's a mindful, sensory practice designed to help you cultivate lasting habits. Every step is deliberately gentle and approachable, making it easy to start, enjoyable to repeat, and deeply rewarding over time. Through small, deliberate actions like selecting your tea, steeping, sipping, savoring, and sharing, you engage your senses, focus your mind, and reinforce the kind of identity you want to embody. In this way, a simple, everyday practice blossoms into a nourishing habit that supports presence, reflection, and personal growth.

How the framework unfolds:

Cue – Selecting your tea
Choosing your tea engages your senses and signals the start of your ritual. It becomes a reminder to pause and be present for yourself.

Routine – Steep, sip, savor
While your tea is steeping, set a small intention to ground yourself in the moment. Both sipping and savoring engage your body and mind, turning ordinary actions into a mindful, nourishing practice. Each small step is thoughtfully manageable, helping the habit settle in naturally.

Reward – Enjoyment and reflection
Every sip offers instant sensory pleasure, while the calm it brings provides clarity and presence. The deepest reward comes when you take time to reflect — savoring the moment not only fills you with greater fulfillment but also guides your mind toward clarity, presence, and focus. This layered reward not only satisfies in the moment but also deepens the habit by linking it to emotional and cognitive benefits.

Reinforcement – Sharing and identity building
Writing down or sharing your tea moment strengthens your sense of identity: "I'm someone who shows up for myself." This self-affirmation creates external reinforcement, adds accountability, and makes the habit more likely to stick.

Each element of this agreeable ritual is rooted in proven behavioral principles:

- *Intentional moments:* Quietly grounding your intention in the moment while your tea steeps can strengthen your focus and guide you toward greater follow-through.
- *Mindfulness grounding:* When you engage your senses, you quiet the noise within, making it easier to stay in the present and in harmony with the moment.
- *Sensory cues:* The comforting warmth, soothing aroma, and feel of tea shift your mental state, inviting calm and clarity.
- *Small, doable actions:* Breaking reflection into small steps makes progress feel steady and achievable.
- *Identity reinforcement:* Celebrating or sharing the habit creates lasting momentum, strengthening your behavior and positive self-image.

Together, these steps turn a simple tea moment into a repeatable, rewarding habit. It's a practice grounded in science but expressed through a calming, nourishing ritual—a gentle way to nurture habits that truly endure.

GENTLY STEP IN AND LET THE PROCESS GUIDE YOU

1. *Select – Create the Cue*

Select your tea with love for the moment you are entering. Let your heart guide you in choosing the blend. The sensory details—aroma, color, texture—act as your cue, signaling the start of your ritual.

2. *Steep – Set Your Intention*

As the tea steeps, enjoy a moment of stillness. This pause is perfect for reflection or for setting an intention.

3. *Sip – Engage Mindfully*

Allow every sip to delight your senses and draw you into the present moment. This mindful attention centers you and pairs calm moments with the clarity you want to nurture, until your brain begins to crave this steady sense of ease.

4. *Savor – Choose a Micro-Action*

During or after sipping, identify one small, easy action you can take that aligns with your intention for the day. This is the moment when you turn your reflection into a tiny, *doable action* you can take today, making it real and achievable. By linking your thought to this small action and then to a positive outcome, you create a gentle habit-building cycle. Choose something easy to increase your chances of following through, helping build momentum and confidence along the way.

5. *Share or Record – Reinforce Identity*
And in the end, write down your intention, or tell a friend or family member about it. This step strengthens consistency and identity, helping you internalize the idea: "I am someone who shows up for myself with reflection and purpose." When you record or share, you add a layer of accountability and self-recognition that supports long-term growth.

You choose an enlivening English Breakfast tea for a pleasant energy boost to start the day. A soft mist drifts upward from the pot, and warmth spirals gently into the room. You carefully scoop the leaves and listen as the water cascades over them. As the tea begins to steep, time slows, drifting calmly like steam from a cup, and your heart opens to your thoughts. Maybe you set an intention. You could ask yourself a gentle question. Or maybe you breathe.

Each sip settles you into the present, and in that time, a tiny thought blooms quietly—a small action you can take today that feels aligned with who you want to be. Before the mug empties, you jot down a word, a phrase, or a small intention. Like a gentle breeze over a quiet lake, nothing is forced, nothing is hurried—everything unfolds in stillness and presence. In just minutes, your tea has become more than a warm drink. It has become a rhythm, a reset, a quiet ritual that gently supports the person you are becoming.

What if every cup of tea became a moment to rewire your habits—to move you closer to the life you want to create? That's the idea behind the Teatimely Habits Method—a mindful framework that turns a simple act into a daily ritual of reflection, alignment, and growth. This is your moment to begin again—one cup, one breath, one intention at a time.

10

Your Cozy Corner of Joy

Home. It is the comforting place that I return to after meeting daily responsibilities. It is my destination for winding down after the spontaneous adventures that life leads me on. Home is the only place where I am free to be myself, surrounded by my favorite things, in the company of loved ones. It is a retreat where I can immerse myself in pleasant pastimes.

Adorned with all the little things that bring me comfort and joy, home is my favorite place. It is here that I unapologetically indulge in the beauty and romance of a tea-scented, flower-filled, rose-colored world. Fragrant with the aroma of chai and lavender, my humble home promises a grand celebration of tea and love. Whimsical tea sets, blushing in pastel hues, meet elegant decor, creating a cozy cottage haven where we can gather and find tranquility. It's a place for moments of sweetness that stir the spirit. A lovely backdrop for warm and cozy experiences. A setting for the fun memories we create. Every space awaits a story. My bookshelf, a most agreeable place to stop by for a pick-me-up, is brimming with beautiful books, gourmet tea, picturesque artwork, and positive messages.

The decorative items that adorn this abode are curated with care. Spaces are thoughtfully designed with consideration for the moments of charm and cheer they will help us create. The aesthetic marries shabby chic and whimsy with a fun and modern take on femininity: lavishly pink with luxurious velvet, ruffles, flowers, lace, and delicate embellishments that speak not just to romantics at heart but also anyone who wants to be surrounded by beauty.

Immersed in my passion for tea and my family's needs, I have created an environment meant to uplift, nourish, relax, and bring cozy comfort. Every moment at home offers an opportunity to revel in the good things in life with those we love.

Create your own beautiful little world, a refuge that is both quaint and pleasant. Creating a happy place at home is about curating your space for joy and personal growth. It is a special place that promotes relaxation and nurtures your well-being. Home is a place to recharge and escape the stresses of daily life. A place to be yourself and unreservedly enjoy doing things that lift your spirits. Whether it's a room or a cozy corner, the goal is to design a space where you feel encouraged to unwind, recharge, and welcome experiences that boost happiness.

A happy place may also be away from home—a nice spot at a park, a café with a peaceful ambiance, or a favorite hiking trail. These are all wonderful. Yet today, I would like you to consider creating a cheery little space at home so that you may awaken to it every day and return to it at the day's end. One's home should be an inviting place of refuge—a retreat that comforts the soul, supports well-being, and brings about serene contentment.

Create an uplifting dwelling that shines with brightness and hope. Beautifying your surroundings is one of the easiest and most immediate ways to brighten your day. A clean, well-organized environment, decorated with little things that make you smile, can promote peace, mental clarity, and positivity. Think about the things that truly bring you joy and what area of your home can be transformed into something special. Design the space to be warm and inspiring. Once you have a fabulous space, use it to engage in pleasant practices that center your mental and emotional well-being.

Reminisce about things that bring you joy. What truly brings you peace and contentment? This requires self-reflection—take time to think about the activities, people, or experiences that make you feel happy and alive. It could be time spent with family and friends, hobbies that you like, or simple moments of quietness enjoyed by yourself. Some people find happiness in being surrounded by nature, while others find joy in creative pursuits like painting or reading.

When identifying what brings you joy, consider moments when you felt fully present and at ease. These experiences are clues to the elements that can shape your happy place. Whether it's the soothing sound of the ocean, the smell of fresh flowers, or certain fabrics and colors, recognizing what makes you feel grounded and happy is the foundation for building your happy place.

Plan to start each dawn in a good environment, waking up to a pleasant space and a sense of coziness. Home is a sanctuary, a place where we seek comfort, rest, and solace from the outside world. Start by choosing a specific spot that feels calming and settles your heart. This could be your bedroom, a small corner of your home, or a quaint outdoor space that welcomes serenity.

Once you have chosen the area, focus on the elements that can enhance the peaceful atmosphere. Soft lighting, such as lamps or fairy lights, can add a sense of warmth and coziness to a room. Simply incorporating natural elements like wood, stone, plants, flowers, rocks, or water features can provide a sense of peacefulness and connect you with nature.

A snug reading nook by a window with plenty of natural light can serve as a charming haven where you can unwind with a good book. A room dedicated to your hobbies or creative pursuits can become a stimulating space where you feel inspired to engross yourself in a fun activity. If you don't have a lot of space, a small corner with a comfy chair, a soft throw, and a few personalized touches can become your escape. Merely arranging your cozy corner of joy with comfortable furniture, soothing colors, and personal items that evoke positive memories can make it a special place to unwind.

Arrange your surroundings to kindle joy and laughter. Are you uplifted by bright, vibrant colors or soothed by neutral tones? Do you find tranquility in a clutter-free, minimalist setting, or do you thrive in spaces filled with character, warmth, and personal items? By identifying these preferences, you can create a space that aligns with your emotional and sensory needs. Whether you enjoy natural light, soft textures, or specific colors, understanding what contributes to your well-being can help you tailor the environment to your unique sense of comfort and happiness.

Allow yourself the pleasure of relaxing in a space radiating with optimism and light. Ambience can play a significant role in shaping your happy place. A calming atmosphere is essential for relaxation and peace. Start by focusing on lighting, color, and scents—elements that can evoke different moods.

LIGHTING

Soft, warm lighting can make a room feel homely and welcoming. You might use lamps, a cascade of little lights, or flameless candles to create a gentle, soothing glow. Let natural light flood the space during the day, as it can help improve mood and provide a sense of openness.

COLOR

Give some thought to the colors you choose for your cozy corner, as they can have a psychological impact. Neutral tones, like soft grays, blues, or whites, can evoke calmness and serenity. If your spirit leans toward vibrancy, consider adding cheerful hues like yellow or turquoise through accents like throw pillows, art, or rugs. Experiment with different colors to see which ones help you feel relaxed and happy.

SCENTS

Essential oils, aromatic candles, and diffusers can fill the area with a soothing fragrance. I have observed that lavender, chamomile, lemon, bergamot, and rose help me relax. Scents are rather personal, though, and you may want to find the one that calms you and warms your heart.

PERSONALIZATION

Bring something of yourself into it. A happy place at home reflects your personality and interests. Personal touches add a sense of ownership and joy to the space. Have fun adding things that make you happy. A favorite artwork, colorful and cheerful décor, comfy fabrics, and inspirational quotes can add a sense of calm, warmth, and optimism to the space.

Surrounding yourself with the lovely little things that make you smile is a simple yet effective way to care for your well-being. Fill your happy place with items that hold positive memories and lift your spirits. This could include:

ARTWORK

Adorn the walls with images that inspire or move your heart—art and photos that spark joy and hold the soft glow of moments past. Whether you like beautiful landscape paintings, chocolate-box images, custom art, or family photos, personal touches make the space feel uniquely yours. A gallery wall of joyful or meaningful pictures that give the space a positive vibe can certainly brighten one's day as well.

TEXTURES

Incorporating soft and inviting textiles can make your spot feel snug and relaxing. Consider adding plush rugs, blankets, or throw pillows to create a physically comforting environment. The tactile sensation of soft materials adds a sense of warmth and security. It can be great to mix and match a variety of materials to create a distinctive space that welcomes you to rest there.

KEEPSAKES

Surround yourself with a collection of meaningful objects—things that remind you of loved ones and fun experiences, evoke happy memories, and highlight achievements. A gift from a good friend, a souvenir from a memorable trip, and a favorite item from childhood are warm, gentle touches that can enhance the emotional comfort and contentment of the space.

LET NATURE IN

Surround yourself with natural beauty. Bringing elements of nature into your home is a fantastic way to create a calming and blissful space. Studies suggest that exposure to nature can reduce stress, improve mood, and boost overall well-being. If you don't have access to an outdoor garden, there are still ways to introduce nature indoors.

INDOOR PLANTS

The presence of nature, even in small forms such as a houseplant or a flower arrangement, can make your day feel brighter. Plants can add a little calmness and life to any space.

NATURAL MATERIALS

Adding materials such as wood, stone, rattan, or seagrass can also foster a sense of peacefulness. Wood furniture, stone vases or decor, and natural woven baskets and trays can add texture and tranquility while connecting the space to nature.

NATURE SOUNDS

For days when you can't get outside, bring the outdoors inside by playing soothing nature sounds. A small sound machine or a playlist of rain, waves, or birdsong can help create a serene atmosphere. A tabletop water fountain can also be relaxing.

FUN ADDITIONS

Think about ways to add playful elements and quirky accessories to your space. Novelty wall décor, funny quotes, unique lamps, and eccentric art are some great options. Fun throw pillows or blankets, cool mugs, and cheerful décor can lighten your space.

> "Fill your home with heart.
> Your home will fill your heart
> with cozy contentment and joy."
>
> ✦✦✦

Keep your happy place nice and tidy. While it is important to decorate your space to enhance your sense of well-being, it is also important to avoid clutter. Simple acts like organizing your dresser or desk, tidying up, and opening windows to let in fresh air and natural light can transform the energy in your home. Style your space thoughtfully—choosing only items that are meaningful and essential to promote relaxation and joy. Keeping your space neat is an essential part of creating and maintaining your happy place. This doesn't mean everything needs to be perfect, but rather that a clean, orderly environment can foster clarity and peace of mind.

Relish activities that bring you joy. Creating a happy place at home is about more than just decorating a space—it's about what you do within that space that makes you happy. Consider dedicating specific areas of your home to specific activities that promote relaxation, happiness, and fulfillment.

Whether it's losing oneself in a beloved book, sipping a cup of tea, writing, baking, painting, making jewelry, working out, or doing yoga, these activities can help create a sense of contentment in your happy place. If possible, integrate these activities into your daily routine, making your home a space that supports your emotional well-being and helps you cultivate joy and satisfaction in your everyday life.

Having a cozy, heartwarming place to return to each day is invaluable. No matter where you go or what adventures you set out on, you have a place to return to. Your happy place is where you free yourself from the weight of the world, unwind, and give yourself time to heal. It's a thoughtfully created haven where you might bask in the understated pleasures of each passing day, and *just be*.

II

The Teapot of Gentle Reminders

In New York, I have my heart set on having a quaint afternoon tea at a charming little tea shop I've heard lovely things about. Yet, today is my birthday, and my husband takes me to Soho for a tea date to celebrate. The gorgeous tearoom, which I previously visited in other cities, is as elaborately decorated as can be. A three-tiered stand offers all manner of temptations, from extravagant pastries savory bites. It is all so exquisite, and my heart overflows with gratitude.

I am, however, more interested in getting outside into the hustle and bustle and watching the world go by. I like sitting on a bench, observing the world, and writing a few sentences that capture the dazzling beauty before my eyes. There are countless people from all walks of life, many of them silently carrying a story you will never fully know.

It makes you realize something valuable: you are not alone in your dreaming, struggling, and blooming. Every person who brushes past you on the sidewalk has endured something. Every heart holds a little world of love, longing, joy, and sorrow. And yet—like you—they still got up this morning. They still made tea (or coffee). They still showed up, and they matter. Everyone matters. You matter because you are here.

Perhaps one day you may find the courage to tell your story, or maybe you will rewrite it. Even if you simply hold onto it gently, know that it matters, and you matter, too.

——— ✦ ———

Happiness is not acquired after a long and tiring quest; it is experienced by brightening one's everyday life with a collection of daily habits that boost joy. An easy way to cultivate more beauty and positivity in your life is by brightening your day with gentle little reminders. These are expressions of warmth that can spark light, inspiration, and contentment. It's a reminder that you matter.

Much like affirmations, the goal is to guide your mind toward positive thinking. The difference is that you don't have to repeat gentle reminders, unless you would like to, of course. Instead, you incorporate them into your daily routine.

Whether you print out a copy and frame it in your room, keep it in your planner or journal, or place it on your desk at work, making them physically visible may be helpful. Perhaps you might even use Post-it notes to stick these nice little reminders in places you are likely to see them. It's also fun to stick them on teabag envelopes so you can read one every time you prepare tea.

LOVELY LITTLE REMINDERS

"I am enough."
Reaffirm your worth. You are amazing, and you don't need to be anything more than you already are.

"It's perfectly okay to be imperfect."
Celebrate your flaws and quirks. Life isn't about striving for perfection; it's about embracing your authentic self.

"This moment is enough."

Remind yourself that you don't need to chase excellence or stress about the future. The present is a gift. Embrace it, and live it with all your heart.

"I have a lot to be grateful for."
Gratitude can shift your mindset and boost joy. Every day, think about (and preferably write down) three things that you are grateful for.

"It's good to take breaks."
Allow yourself a few moments of self-care to rest and recharge throughout the day. This can be through a quiet tea break, a quick walk, or gentle stretching.

"I deserve to be happy."
Remind yourself that you are worthy of joy and deserve it every single day.

"Stop and smell the roses."
Intentionally slow down and see the beauty around you, taking time to savor life's simple pleasures.

"Laugh often."

Laughter lightens daily loads and can instantly boost your mood. Read jokes, watch a funny video, or talk to a friend who makes you laugh.

"I am in control of my attitude."

Remind yourself that even though you can't control many of the things that happen each day, you have control over how you process and respond to it.

"It will be ok."

No matter what the day presents to you, remind yourself that you will get through it and that things will be okay.

"Celebrate small victories."

Praise your progress, no matter how little it seems. Bigger things are achieved through many small steps.

"Love makes the world a better place."

Love yourself, others, plants, animals, and the earth. Cherishing and nurturing love make the world more beautiful and life more fulfilling.

"I will spread kindness."

Remind yourself to infuse your day with goodness by uplifting others. Small acts of kindness give you a sense of purpose and contentment.

"Today, I choose joy."

Every morning, deliberately decide to find joy in whatever comes your way. Strive to focus on the positives. Aspire to meet each day with optimism.

> **SIP OF INSPIRATION**
>
> Consider writing affectionate reminders on little pieces of paper and placing them in "The Teapot of Gentle Reminders." Grab one for an instant boost.

Rather than focusing on external sources of happiness, look for ways to create moments of joy and positivity in your everyday life. Having gentle little reminders to uplift you can be an effective way to boost positive thoughts. Which reminders truly resonate with you today? Perhaps you could come up with a few to add to the list.

12

The Gratitude Habit

Gratitude is the delicate bloom of a rose in the garden of the heart, beautifying your world and adding a delicately sweet fragrance. Every time you experience this contented, appreciative feeling, another blossom blooms. Let your heart be so full that you see beauty all around you.

When we embrace gratitude, we adopt a way of life, a way of seeing the world, and a way of processing the events of daily life. Research suggests that there are many potential benefits to cultivating gratitude in your life regularly. It may have a strong and consistent association with reduced stress and an improvement in physical and mental health. In addition, it can help us feel more positive emotions and appreciate the good experiences in our lives.

Gratitude is when your heart quietly celebrates the blessings that grace your day. It is the contentment of the soul. Identify your little joys, appreciate them, and celebrate them gladly. To live in gratitude is to recognize that each day is a gift, and every moment a quiet blessing not to be overlooked. It is to know that the people in your life are gems, and that every time a heart connects with your heart, a chapter of your story is beginning. A smile becomes sunshine that brightens your day, the arms that embrace you become your greatest treasures, and the little things become *everything*.

Studies indicate that gratitude can help boost health, build resilience in tough times, and strengthen relationships with others. Recognize the value of your blessings—no matter how small they may seem. In the bigger picture, it's often these little gifts that bring the most joy and wonder to our lives. It is gratitude that frees our hearts from less agreeable sentiments and inspires us to focus on the gifts of ordinary days, helping us embrace a true, lasting happiness.

What, then, are things to be grateful for? Joy does not always present itself in grandeur, but in the ordinary moments of everyday life. Gratitude is contentment with not what was or what could be, but with what *is*. Waking up to a new day with new experiences and enjoyments destined for you is one very good reason to start your day with gratitude. A supportive friend, the company of a loved one, a calm moment with a warm mug of tea, a pleasant afternoon, an interesting project, and an act of kindness are just a few things to appreciate.

Brimming with "Things to be Grateful for Every Day" is my daily gratitude checklist, here to inspire you to hold dear the many simple pleasures that life may present to you each day.

THINGS TO BE GRATEFUL FOR EVERYDAY

- ☐ A New Day
  Be grateful for the gift of waking up to another day—another chance to live, love, and grow.

- ☐ Your Health
  Appreciate your breath, your heartbeat, your senses—the miracles that keep you connected to life.

- ☐ A Cup of Tea
  A single cup of tea can hold warmth, comfort, peace, and joy.

- ☐ Family
  Be grateful for those who stand by you, your forever team, bound by love.

- ☐ Sight
  The ability to see is a daily blessing. Look around—there's beauty everywhere.

- ☐ Your Unique Gifts
  You are special. Celebrate your strengths, and everything that makes you, *you*.

- ☐ Acts of Kindness
  A kind deed can lift spirits—yours and another's.

- ☐ Clean Water
  Access to clean drinking water is a blessing many don't have. Cherish it.

- ☐ Sunshine & Rain
  The sun brightens our world. Rain rejuvenates the earth.

- ☐ Parents
  They brought you into this world and nurtured you with love and care.

- ☐ Friends
  Like flowers in the garden of life, they bring connection, beauty, and joy.

- ☐ Time
  It's a valuable gift. Spend it meaningfully, and savor every minute.

- ☐ Fashion
  Dressing up is a daily celebration of self-expression and beauty.

- ☐ Peace
  Peace in your home, in relationships, and within is a most prized treasure.

- ☐ Your Mind
  Your thoughts shape your world. With it, you learn, solve, create, and dream.

- ☐ Sweet Treats
  Cakes, cookies, confections—it's the little things that make life sweeter.

- ☐ Challenges

They shape you. With every struggle, you grow stronger and wiser.

- Love
  The powerful, bejeweled bond that connects hearts and souls.

- Self-Belief
  Be your own lifelong friend. Trust yourself and walk forward confidently.

- Knowledge
  You have endless opportunities to learn and grow—books, podcasts, courses, and more.

- Laughter
  A melody from the soul that brings lightness to the heart.

- Wisdom
  With wisdom comes the understanding that gratitude deepens life's meaning.

- Nature's Beauty
  The world is adorned with natural wonders

for you to see and enjoy. Trees, trails, sunshine—go outside and breathe it in.

- ☐ Sunsets
  They remind us to slow down and cherish the close of each day.

- ☐ Gardens
  Flowers, trees, and greenery add peace and splendor to our everyday surroundings.

- ☐ Playfulness
  Never forget the joy of being playful. Life's most magical moments often begin with laughter.

- ☐ Home
  It's your sanctuary—a place to rest, reflect, and be yourself.

- ☐ Your Partner
  The one who loves you deeply and makes your world richer just by being in it.

- ☐ Food
  Every meal is a celebration of flavor, nourishment, and enjoyment.

- ☐ Bath & Shower
  Let aromatic soap and warm water wash away the day. It's a nourishing act of self-care.

- ☐ Books
  A good book transports you, enlightens you, and fills your world with wonder.

- ☐ Rest
  Sleep renews your body, mind, and soul. Welcome it with gratitude each night.

- ☐ The Moon & Stars
  Their quiet presence at night whispers that it's time to dream again.

- ☐ Your Life
  Above all, be thankful for this life—yours to shape, celebrate, and enjoy each day.

Gratitude is like the hour of day when the light softens, and everything we cherish is bathed in quiet gold—a gentle reminder of all that is well.

> ### SIP OF INSPIRATION
> What are the most important blessings that grace your day? Write your own daily checklist. Consider keeping it close by for reflection.

13

The Habit of Appreciating the Little Things

When you begin your journey of cultivating gratitude, you may discover that it is more than a practice reserved for certain days of the week—it makes space for itself within your routine. Gratitude is the habit of consistently appreciating the beauty and blessings that are present in your daily life. It's about celebrating the little things that spark joy. Purposely enrich your day with small felicities that make your heart happy, ensuring that, amid the mundane, you brighten your day with small uplifting moments.

When you choose to focus on life's little wonders with true affection, you begin to ease your journey and open the door to greater gratitude and contentment. Settle into a pattern of deliberately basking in the small moments of splendor and happiness nestled in the mundane. It is the appreciation of the magic found in the small moments that can lead to greater overall happiness.

Through this brilliant practice, you can brighten your outlook, shift your perspective, and stay focused on the good things in life.

HOW TO PRACTICE GRATITUDE

Practicing thankfulness involves recognizing the value in both the tangible and intangible aspects of your life—the visible and the unseen. It's about cultivating a spirit of appreciation that extends beyond the material things and embracing life's more delicate offerings. The connections we share, the lessons of experience, the quiet stirrings of emotion, and even the challenges we face bring depth to our experience. Gratitude is not solely reserved for days enhanced with comfort and joy; rather, it's about searching for the silver lining and finding something to appreciate, even on the most challenging of days.

As you embark upon your journey of gratitude, endeavor to gently redirect your gaze toward the soft glow of daily blessings that illuminate your life. Think about the tender moments of lightness and loveliness that beautified your day. The small triumphs, invaluable comforts, and unexpected joys are all worthy of gracious acknowledgement. What brought you calmness or mirth today? What simple pleasures did you enjoy? Take note of these moments, recognizing how they enrich and give meaning to your everyday life.

To make gratitude a meaningful part of your daily routine, it's essential to find a practice that truly resonates with you, one that you can look forward to. Make time to experience the things you're thankful for, allowing yourself the treat of indulging in them regularly amid the everyday. Perhaps, in the stillness of morning, you might pause to linger with the singing of the birds, the cool breath of dawn upon your skin, the comforting warmth of a well-steeped cup of tea, or the first bite of breakfast.

You may enjoy more of your simple luxuries, like wearing clothes that make you feel comfortable and happy. If the beauty of nature brings your heart ease, let time spent amidst trees, flowers, and open skies become a special part of your routine. Above all, cherish the majesty of your most beloved relationships. Connecting with the people who are close to your heart through a message, a call, or in the warmth of shared presence can bring profound feelings of thankfulness and contentment.

You can gracefully welcome gratitude into your life through many meaningful pathways. With each new dawn, set the intention to appreciate the little things in life that so often go unnoticed—the simple pleasures and everyday treasures. To begin the morning in a spirit of gratitude is to bestow upon the hours that follow a sense of peace and contentment. An effective way to remind yourself is to adorn your space with inspirational art featuring a gratitude affirmation or quote, and to read it during your morning routine.

And, as the day draws to its gentle close, take but a moment to reflect upon the lovely little things that have graced your path. Such a practice carries the power to help you cultivate deep, lasting contentment. Morning gratitude, gratitude tea time, and evening journaling are all agreeable ways to embrace appreciation each day.

TINY JOYS, COLLECTED DAILY

What, then, is a gratitude journal? It is a delicate archive of the heart's most cherished remembrances and the blessings that grace each day. More than a diary, it is a special place for the most prized sentiments—exclusively those favorable ones that begin to shift your perspective toward positivity, changing your view on life. Your book of thankful reflections is a quiet reminder to muse upon and collect moments the soul recalls with fondness. It's the heart's treasure box in which one tenderly gathers glimmers of peace, beauty, kindness, and joy so they are safely kept. It is a reflection of the soul's contentment.

The keeping of such a journal helps us become more aware of the abundance in our lives. A gratitude journal inspires you to cultivate the art of appreciating small moments and the sumptuousness of life's simple pleasures. On the path you're walking, the mindful habit of noting small joys can nurture a more grounded and grateful way of being. As evening falls, endeavor to write down at least three wonderful things or moments that have gained your appreciation. Turn your journal into a compilation of tiny joys, collected daily.

It is the small, often-overlooked blessings that we should be grateful for, as these are the ones that weave wonder into the ordinary. Reminisce about the simple pleasures that life has gifted you a chance to luxuriate in today. Is it the first sip of your morning tea or coffee, a kind word from a loved one, the feeling of a small hand in your hand, or a serene moment in the garden? Give thought to the little things that made today a *good* day. You could also be grateful for what you learn, the challenges you overcome, and the small triumphs. The nice people in your life and the heartwarming moments you enjoy with them are also to be remembered most affectionately.

Journaling can open your eyes to the beauty that quietly perseveres around you. It can help you appreciate the good that already embellishes your everyday life. The practice of keeping a diary of daily thanks can inspire a positive habit of noticing the good and appreciating the gentle joys that blossom between heartbeats.

14

Daily Gratitude Affirmations

Opening your eyes to the sight of comfort and home, the whisper of your breath, and the rhythm of your heart should be the reason you awaken with a feeling of gratitude every day. You were *chosen* to live another day. You were given the chance to enjoy the magic and the beauty of this world today. Every day is a gift—be grateful for each day you are blessed with.

Did you know that ten minutes a day can change the way you view the world? Starting each morning with gratitude can guide one's perspective toward positivity and happiness. When we transform our mindset, we can transform our day. While life sparkles with many sweet luxuries that we should regard with deepest appreciation, there are fourteen things that I express sincere thanks for every day. Let us begin our day with powerful gratitude affirmations.

Have you ever wondered how positive thinking can change your life? Research on positive affirmations suggests that this simple practice can rewire the brain to think more positively and improve well-being. This gentle practice may help boost self-perception, reduce stress, and increase confidence.

I will list each affirmation and share a beautiful thought for you to reflect on. You may find it helpful to incorporate these inspirational phrases into your morning routine, repeating them silently or aloud. Over time, this practice can help you cultivate more gratitude in your everyday life.

I am grateful for a new day.
Today is a new day. New opportunities, new experiences, and new reasons to smile await you.

I am grateful for tea.
That first cup of comfort in the morning that lifts your spirits and empowers you to start the day.

I am grateful for my health.
Feel your heartbeat, focus on your breath. Your mind has the power to think beautiful thoughts. Your heart

is a gift that helps create beautiful emotions.

I am grateful for my home.
The familiar objects. The comfort. The place where you are free to be yourself. It reminds you that you belong somewhere. No matter where you go or what adventures you set out on, you have a place to return to.

I am grateful for my capabilities.
You are special, my dear friend, and today, you should be grateful for your skills, strengths, and abilities.

I am grateful for time.
Time to sit and marvel at the beauty around you. Time to eat. Time to spend with a loved one. Time is invaluable. Enjoy it thoughtfully.

I am grateful for opportunities.
Whatever the day may present, it is an opportunity to learn, to grow. Embrace every trial and task, for they have helped you become the strong and amazing person you are today and will become tomorrow.

I am grateful for love.

Self-love. The love you feel for family or friends. Your beloved. Love for nature. Love for all living things. Love is a bejeweled emotion as pure as a blossoming flower. The most precious gift worthy of gratitude.

I am grateful for food.
It nourishes us. It lifts our spirits. It brings us together and is a simple yet memorable way to enjoy life.

I am grateful for water.
Clean drinking water is a luxury that should never be taken for granted.

I am grateful for family and friends.
They are the everlasting source of unconditional love, care, and support on your journey.

I am grateful for everyday blessings.
It is the little things that make life beautiful. Measure happiness by counting the number of things in your daily life that bring you joy.

I am grateful for the beauty of nature.
Stop and smell the roses. The world is your

wonderland, with beauty at every turn. Nature nourishes us, it soothes us, it brightens our day and beautifies our world.

I am grateful to be alive.
Life is irreplaceable. In little ways, celebrate life every day.

> **SIP OF INSPIRATION**
> What are some gratitude affirmations that resonate with you? How do these personally meaningful words shape your energy for the hours ahead?

15

Steep. Savor. Soften.

The world, I feel, has often urged me to pursue more than I need: more goals, more efficiency, more achievement. Growing up in an underprivileged immigrant family, I have often found myself succumbing to its every push by working from one morning until almost the next. Years passed in this manner, with the persistent beauty that flourishes in my life going uncelebrated.

I soon discovered that so much of what truly lifts my spirits is neither grand nor is it in a faraway land. It's subtle. It's close by. Accessible. It's the little things. Oh, how easy it is to be consumed by things that shimmer and shine—the dreams we chase, the milestones we set out in pursuit of achieving. Yet, upon the achievement of each, there exists an emptiness that can only be filled by the joy of life's true beauty.

Although I had a lot and indulged fully, I did not experience the same deeply restorative contentment one feels while living life in the embrace of the simple pleasures, free of luxury brands and designer trends. I found myself slowing my pace, tuning into the depth of ordinary moments, and accepting wholeheartedly the humble gifts life bestows upon us each day.

I began to pause—steeping a cup of tea and savoring each sip—softening the edges of the day. A warm cup held in both hands on a quiet morning. The glimmer of gilded afternoon light, streaming through the curtains. The sound of trees dancing in the cold wind of a summer night. The enchanting fragrance of red roses—I stop to breathe it in.

The ordinary wonders of life bring with them a deeper, lasting peace, a contentment that hugs the soul. Achievements can't always replicate this serene, fulfilling feeling. Surely, there is something rather gratifying about immersing yourself in the modest pleasures—not merely passing through them, but actually making them a special part of the day.

I daresay enjoying the little things is, in its own unassuming way, a celebration of life itself. A tea party to show reverence for the life I'm living right now, just as it is. Of course, it does not mean that I will not dream or hope for more—rather, it simply means that I'm learning to let happiness bloom from within the life I am already blessed with.

Throughout my wanderings, I've learned that peace and happiness often dwell not in the achievement of goals, nor at the arrival of destinations, but in the moments of stillness in between. Life doesn't have to be extraordinary to be beautiful. Often, it's in the small, unassuming moments that contentment gently blooms. By embracing positive habits daily and adorning your routine with them, you can uncover more joy in the life you *already* have.

It is the quiet moments—softened by the sweet melodies of laughter, wrapped in gentle comforts, and touched by love's quiet magic—that linger longest in our memory. Start measuring happiness not by the number of things you own nor by the sum of your achievements, but by the quantity of things in your daily life that bring you calmness and joy.

Rejoice in the little things often, pouring love and attention into the ordinary. Start finding happiness in everyday moments, treasuring the tender details of life. Instead of focusing primarily on big accomplishments, purchases, or events, shift your perspective on success and happiness. Constantly chasing bigger milestones in pursuit of happiness can, unfortunately, lead to a feeling of "not enough." Finding joy in the routine, however, can lead to a deep sense of contentment and satisfaction in your day-to-day life. By enjoying everyday blessings, you create a richer, more fulfilling experience of life. Each day holds something of quiet value, and in noticing it, you may find your sense of happiness gently deepened.

Material objects are temporary distractions that can come between you and joy. Putting one's merriment on hold until a much-desired commodity is acquired can potentially waste the valuable time between wanting and obtaining. Worldly things so often lose their luster. They are temporary temptations that shine briefly and then fade once acquired, leaving one in pursuit of the next thing.

Attaching your heart to temporary gratifications can ultimately lead to a feeling of emptiness inside. If you are unhappy because you cannot obtain the things you want, this is an opportunity to learn how to embrace simplicity, making the most of life's sweet little luxuries.

You can work hard to acquire the finest things, but a harsh reality is that there are no guarantees in life. What good are money and possessions then, if you did not enjoy many a day with the people you love? Life is about having as many happy experiences as possible in a limited amount of time. Let your wealth be made of moments of love, laughter, adventure, comfort, and peace.

A life in which one celebrates what is already present can be full of beauty and tranquility. The first step on this path involves thinking about your blessings, privileges, and everyday indulgences. Reflect on your lifestyle and recognize all the amenities you enjoy daily. Chances are that you are living rather well. Many people in this world may never know the comforts that are yours. Instead of saying "I want this," start saying "I have this." Appreciate your blessings by acknowledging their positive impact on your day.

A joyful lifestyle does not demand wealth, status, or accolades. It merely requests intention, an unguarded heart, and presence. Amidst the rush, we slow down. Instead of hearing, we truly listen. Instead of existing, we thoroughly soak in the beauty of each moment. In doing so, we discover the richness that quietly presents itself within the routine. Being able to find beauty in life's most sensible offerings is special. The little things bring a beautiful kind of joy—not the kind that sparkles then fades, but rather, the kind that becomes a quiet, daily glimmer that dependably brightens each day.

It's the little things that linger through all of life's phases, through times good and bad. The soothing effect of the scent of lavender, the sunshine that fulfills its promise of returning, the pages of the book that take you on an adventure—no matter what life may bring or take, the simple pleasures remain. Remember to stir tiny joys into your day.

Acknowledge your source of happiness. Instead of delaying joy until you reach a distant milestone, learn to celebrate life in little ways, all along the way. An uplifting morning routine, an exciting hobby, or a good song on the radio can all be sources of joy if you approach them with a grateful heart. Make a list of the little things that bring you joy. Determine what your life's sweet little luxuries are. Equate happiness to the simple pleasures that uplift you, and start enjoying them every day.

How much contentment do you derive from spending time with your loved ones? Or listening to the unbounded giggle of a child? How do you feel when you are eating a really delicious meal in good company? What brings you true happiness is likely to be found through love, laughter, and connection. Cherish these often, for they are not so far in the future, nor do they require spending a small fortune. Don't let these joys pass by because you are too stressed out about upgrading a gadget or buying a trending luxury good. The cherished moments that you will remember when you are taking your last breath won't be about the big purchase you made, but rather, about the unforgettable memories you made with loved ones.

In the midst of daily chaos, seeking comfort from the everyday pleasures can be healing. It's familiar. It's there. No matter what the day may bring to us, there is still a chance to turn toward the little things for comfort and joy.

The first breeze of fresh morning air. A favorite hearty meal. Taking a warm, fragrant shower. Returning to a favorite chair to relax with a steaming cup of comfort after a long day. Having some quiet time to sit alone and journal in the evening. These joys are accessible. They are yours. Recognizing the positive impact they have on your everyday life can help you become more grateful for them.

And yet, how often do we forget that our collection of achievements, wealth, position, or fancy objects does not simply define happiness? It is the accumulation of small moments of bloom and bliss that ultimately define our contentment. We might forget the exact day that we received a raise, signed an important contract, or bought a designer handbag. Yet, we so fondly remember the big family dinner filled with good food, laughter, and cheerful connection. We reminisce about the warm smile silently exchanged with a significant other. We vividly remember bedtime stories told to those little loves with twinkling eyes and jolly smiles. We might recall the first new bloom of spring in the garden, the summer adventure, the family getaway, and autumn's last leaves.

Life has openheartedly given you an abundance of gifts to unwrap every day. Think about the lovely things that make you smile and warm your heart. Write a list of one hundred simple things that make you happy. I would like to share with you my list of one hundred uplifting things. Which ones brighten your day?

100 LITTLE THINGS FOR INSTANT JOY

1. Waking up to a bright, sunny morning
2. Starting my day with a cup of tea
3. Helping someone in need
4. A cool, refreshing breeze on my face
5. A hug from a loved one
6. Cotton candy at a carnival

7. Hot cocoa on a cold day
8. Fresh tomatoes from the garden
9. Birdsong
10. Taking pictures of beautiful places
11. Coming home after a trip
12. Starting a new hobby
13. Finishing a project I worked hard on
14. A clean kitchen
15. Receiving flowers
16. Early morning mist
17. Nostalgic treats
18. Cuddling
19. Walking through grass barefoot
20. Getting lost in an engrossing book
21. Hearing good news
22. Finding money I forgot I had
23. Tea parties
24. A box of chocolates
25. The smell of rain
26. Saying "I love you"
27. Cozy blankets
28. A glass of cold water on a hot day
29. Receiving a compliment on my outfit
30. A walk in nature
31. A warm shower

32. A good night's sleep
33. Spontaneous adventures
34. The smell of freshly cut lemons and oranges
35. Finding the perfect parking spot
36. Tea shops and bakeries
37. Freshly baked bread
38. The sound of trees blowing in the wind
39. Movie nights
40. Sunlight streaming through the window
41. Seeing the flowers in my garden bloom
42. Wearing cozy socks
43. Finding a great deal or discount
44. Random acts of kindness
45. Feeding birds and other animals
46. Sitting by a fireplace
47. The night sky twinkling with stars
48. Noticing something beautiful
49. Laughing so hard my stomach hurts
50. Road trips
51. The beach
53. Listening to waves or the sound of rain
54. The look and smell of old books
55. Writing in a gratitude journal
56. Decorating
57. Sharing food

58. A clean room
59. A neatly made bed with lots of pretty pillows
60. The first bite of my favorite food
61. Receiving a handwritten card
62. Feeling grateful
63. Holding a baby
64. Having a positive impact on someone
65. Looking through old photos
66. A big family dinner
67. Being appreciated
68. Being outside on a day with perfect weather
69. Sharing a memory with someone
70. Solving a problem
71. Wearing my favorite clothes
72. Seeing a loved one after time apart
73. Dancing like nobody's watching
74. Wearing something new
75. Fairytales
76. Watching a sunset or sunrise
77. Knowing that I am loved
78. Being present in the moment
79. Family gatherings full of laughter
80. Rewatching a favorite TV show
81. Beautiful old buildings
82. Fireworks

83. Ice cream
84. The feeling of sunlight on my face
85. Receiving an unexpected gift
86. Holding a warm drink with both hands
87. Watching children play and giggle
88. Feeling content and not needing anything
89. Watering the plants in the garden
90. Cooking a new dish that turns out delicious
91. Doing something creative
92. Feeling high-spirited after exercising
93. Learning something new
94. Playing games with my family
95. Watching movies I watched as a child
96. The smell of cookies baking
97. Making someone laugh
98. Freshly baked scones
99. Giving a gift
100. Waking up to the sound of a gentle rain

Acknowledging the simple things that make you happy is a gift in itself. You truly triumph once you start incorporating these joys into your life regularly. Next to each one, write an action that you can take to allow yourself the chance to experience them more often.

Next to "Laughing so hard my stomach hurts," I will write: *Watch thirty minutes of comedy every Friday.* For "Being outside on a day with perfect weather," I will write: *Take a quick walk on a beautiful day, twice a week.* To enjoy more "Tea parties," I will host one twice a year—once on Mother's Day and again in December.

Think about how many things from your list you can enjoy every day. How many can you experience each week? Try to maximize the number of little things you take pleasure in. For ultimately, the one who curates the richest collection of small, beautiful moments of joy may be the one who feels the quiet calm of a life well-loved.

Discover more treasured trifles of daily life you can take pleasure in. I always keep my heart open for new and old joys. There's something magical about revisiting the small joys of our childhood. Whether it's a favorite treat, an old TV show, or a setting that once felt like the best place in the world, those sweet morsels of bliss have a way of wrapping us in loving warmth. It's the timeless joy of nostalgia, reminding us of much simpler times when happiness came in small parcels like little glimmers of wonder.

For me, collecting stickers was one such treat. Whimsical designs, cute prints, and entire sticker books with cheerful artwork were among my humble yet profound wells of joy. I quietly carried that enjoyment with me through the years, tucking my collection away like a secret treasure buried in a box deep in my closet.

Now that two little hearts in my life who light up at the sight of stickers, I have happily found a valid reason to return to that quaint joy. I no longer collect pages upon pages or entire sticker books—but rather, a single, pretty sheet at a time. Each twee piece of art feels like a tiny prize, something lovely and full of promise. It's not about the size of the thing, but about the spark of joy it brings.

Beautiful stationery is another classic joy that I am revisiting. The satisfaction of taking time to write a thoughtful note on decorated paper carefully is another charming pleasure I have rediscovered. It allows me to express gratitude and embrace kindness by sending someone tender words of positivity.

> **SIP OF INSPIRATION**
>
> Measure happiness by counting the number of little things and delicate joys in your daily life that fill you with calm and contentment.

Let us slow down and fully enjoy the sweetness quietly hidden in everyday moments. The still morning blooming into bustle and life. Something amusing that comes up unexpectedly and makes you laugh. The comforting scent of your favorite person. The tenderness scintillating in a loved one's eyes when you both exchange a smile. The evening light—a gentle reminder that the day is nearing its end and it's time to care for yourself.

Life is about savoring little joys in tiny teaspoons, everyday magic in small, sweet servings. Let the ordinary things make your heart full. After all, these are not really the little things. They are *everything*.

16

Where Does Joy Hide on Mondays?

Each day presents us with many opportunities to seek out loveliness and bliss. Yet, we are often so deeply engrossed in our responsibilities that we forget to notice the daily beauty in our lives. Curating a collection of tiny uplifting habits in your routine can make joy more achievable. Start measuring happiness in moments, adding to your schedule simple pleasures to enjoy every single day.

Seek your fulfilment not in wealth or praise but in the quiet blessings that neither fade nor tarnish, in the beauty of contented living. The sweetness of possessions is but fleeting, while the magic of memories we create becomes stronger over a lifetime. Let the true measure of joy be the experiences we gather. You don't need to have a lot of money to have a good time. Instead of taking a trip to Hawaii, plan a picnic on the beach. Hawaii can wait, but a fun day at the beach is an opportunity that is nearby and waiting.

Rather than shopping for products or services you don't really need, consider saving that money and using it to pay for a vacation or a mini getaway. The merriment you experience with your favorite people can last much longer than the satisfaction of a new product, *unless* it is a small appliance like an ice cream maker! Setting aside extra money for products that make waffles, fondue, popcorn, mini donuts, or cotton candy can transform your home into an enjoyable space, bringing joy to everyone time and time again. Joy grows best where laughter lives and the fun never ends.

Whether it is connecting with loved ones at a dinner party or sleeping under the sun at the beach, we all have little gems of happiness that bring us greater contentment than material things. Find more gentle pleasures of the heart to enjoy, for these are the lovely things you will likely cherish throughout your life. Being the tea enthusiast that I am, I keep a special black tea on hand to treat myself once a week. It is something simple but pleasant, a planned moment of joy that I can look forward to.

Think about the small pleasures you can look forward to each day of the week. Consider setting a day to watch your favorite television show or to eat your favorite food. Choose a day to enjoy your favorite tea or coffee. Unveil that velvety, decadent chocolate that almost makes you feel guilty whenever you indulge in it. Plan to reward yourself with the little things regularly.

In the hurried world that we live in, it is easy to overlook the gentle joys that surround us. We might be focused on bigger goals, deadlines, and tasks, forgetting to appreciate life's tender blessings. Finding ways to enjoy the simple pleasures is a practice that can help create a more fulfilling and meaningful lifestyle. By intentionally focusing on the everyday moments that bring us peace, joy, gratitude, and satisfaction, we can cultivate a more mindful, present existence.

Sip the beauty around you to soften the passing hour. An easy way to embrace this mindset is by finding a moment of contentment to savor every day. Pause daily, and, with a willing heart, revel in the simple joys of beauty and calm that life bestows.

LITTLE PLEASURES TO ENJOY EACH DAY OF THE WEEK

Monday: Morning Positive-Tea
Starting the week can feel daunting for many, but you can transform Monday morning into a positive beginning. Take time to make a perfect cup of tea or coffee and sit quietly to enjoy it. The warmth, aroma, and the simple act of sitting down to sip your favorite drink while lingering in the moment can provide a gentle start to the week. Whether it's the first sip or the quiet time to yourself before the day begins, enjoying this simple pleasure can set a positive tone for the rest of the day. Repeat positive morning affirmations to start your day with bright, beautiful energy.

Tuesday: A Walk in Nature
Taking a walk in nature encourages us to step outside and appreciate the beauty around us. It could include a peaceful stroll through a park, a quick walk around one's neighborhood, or an energizing hike through the woods. Nature always has a special way of grounding us. The fresh air, the beautiful greenery, and the sound of birds singing and leaves rustling can help reduce stress and clear our minds. On Tuesdays, try to find a little time to connect with nature. Notice something beautiful. A flower. A leaf. A cloud shaped like a dinosaur.

Wednesday: A Pampering Bath

By the time Wednesday rolls around, the week may feel like it's dragging. It's a good time to hit the reset button. Take time to pamper yourself with a warm, relaxing bath. I enjoy filling the tub with bubbles and the enchanting fragrance of lavender, chamomile, bergamot, lemon, or rose. Dropping a handful of silky rose petals into the bath can add a special touch.

Be present in this moment. Feel the comfort of the cozy water enveloping your body. Let the scents soothe you and transport you to a realm of elevated relaxation. Let go of any lingering stress from the week. A bit of self-care and pampering can help you recharge. These small but caring acts let you enjoy the rest and joy that are often overlooked in a hectic week.

Thursday: A Kind Compliment

On Thursdays, reserve a moment to spread kindness by giving someone a thoughtful compliment. It could be a colleague, friend, family member, or even a stranger you encounter during your day. Quick and simple, giving a compliment can brighten someone's day and give you a deep sense of satisfaction, knowing you lifted their spirits. Acknowledging the good in others is a thoughtful act that brings warmth to both you and those around you.

Friday: Treating Yourself
Friday marks the end of the work week and the start of the weekend—it is a day to celebrate. Make it a tradition to treat yourself to something that brings you happiness. This could mean enjoying a favorite dessert, watching an enthralling movie or favorite TV show, or dedicating time to a hobby you love. The pleasure comes not from the grandness of the act, but from taking the time to reward yourself and to enjoy something small that feels indulgent. By making space for simple joys on Fridays, you can mark the beginning of a wonderful weekend.

Saturday: Connecting with Loved Ones
On Saturdays, plan to nurture the relationships that lift you. Enjoying a simple conversation over a meal, sharing a laugh, and spending quality time together can create deep feelings of gratitude and contentment. Fun family outings, an adventure with a loved one, or catching up with a friend over dinner can all bring moments of joy. Weekdays can get busy, but making space for genuine connection on weekends is one of the best ways to let happiness bloom. Sharing heart-lifting experiences with

your favorite people is one of the best ways to strengthen your emotional bonds and create lasting memories.

Sunday: Enjoy Simple Pleasures
On Sunday, let us delight in the beauty and romance of a tea-scented, flower-filled, rose-colored world. Buy flowers for yourself, and head home for a lovely day of relaxation. Slow down. Steep a cup of aromatic tea and savor each sip from a nice cup. With a grateful heart, see the beauty that quietly persists all around. Watch something that makes you happy. A show about gardening or traveling to a beautiful place can certainly be a pleasure to watch.

You can also read an uplifting book that is full of good thoughts, knowledge, inspiration, or adventure. It's nice to lose oneself in lighthearted content, letting worries drift away and encouraging positivity. Shift your perspective toward happiness and possibility as you prepare to start a new week.

> "What is the secret to a day well-lived, day after day? A little joy to look forward to, a quiet moment to delight in it, and an open heart ready to embrace the magic of it."

✦✦✦

It is the little things in life that are often the most meaningful, and we have to consciously and consistently prioritize small joys. By embracing small pleasures each day of the week, we can live more fully in the present and find contentment in the everyday experiences that make life wondrous. From savoring your morning tea slowly to making time for softer, heart-to-heart moments, each day offers opportunities to enjoy the little things that matter. Joy is a habit. Practice daily.

You deserve joy, even on Mondays. When you begin to appreciate those humble, often overlooked moments, you can cultivate a more balanced, mindful, joyful existence. Look forward to your daily pleasures each week, for oftentimes, happiness can be discovered in small, fragrant blossoms of delight.

SIP OF INSPIRATION

Ask yourself this: Is there space in my day where I could invite more joy? What is one simple thing that I can do each day on *purpose* to spark happiness?

17

Daily Habits of Joy Calendar

I first created a Daily Habits of Joy Calendar during a particularly vulnerable and difficult year of my life. It changed everything, and I found myself holding on to this treasurable practice month after month. This special calendar is meant to introduce small moments of gladness into your daily routine, giving you something uplifting to look forward to and enjoy every single day. Let it be your gentle invitation to slow down, savor the little things, and choose joy, *on purpose*, again and again. You probably won't feel joyful every day, and that's okay. Intentional joy is not about forcing happiness, but about being open to planting seeds of joy *when* and *where* it can grow.

If there is just one thing you take away from this book, let it be this: cultivate a habit of intentional joy, daily. Be deliberate about finding moments of beauty and bliss in your life. Make it a daily discipline with the Daily Habits of Joy Calendar.

To begin, we must first create a Daily Habits of Joy Menu. It includes small, manageable actions we plan to carefully weave into our daily routine to boost happiness and a positive mindset. The goal is to try one a day, *on purpose*. This list is not the same as the "100 Things for Instant Joy" list shared earlier in the book, although that can be referred to for inspiration. The Daily Habits of Joy Menu includes simple, actionable items, things you can *do daily* to spark a small uplifting moment of joy. The list is divided into several categories, allowing us to pick different ones for various days of the week. I'll share my joy menu below. What lifts my spirits might be different from what brightens your day, so I encourage you to add your own personalized items to the list to make it yours. If you are familiar with my planner, please note that this joy menu is a little different from the more comprehensive version in the *Daily Habits of Joy Planner: A 90-Day Guided Journal for Building Habits of Self-Care, Calm, and Everyday Joy*.

DAILY HABITS OF JOY MENU

Quick Joys (*1–5 minutes*)
- Repeat powerful, positive morning affirmations.
- Step outside for fresh air and take 5 to 10 slow, deep breaths.
- Pause, look outside your window, and notice something beautiful.
- Sip your favorite warm drink (tea, coffee, water, hot cocoa) mindfully, one slow sip at a time.
- Watch an inspirational or funny video.
- Look into your own eyes, smile, and affirm, "You've got this, and you're doing great."
- Write 3 things you're grateful for right now.
- Do a happy dance.
- _____
- _____
- _____
- _____
- _____
- _____

Creative Joys
- Write a poem, short story, or essay.

- Take a picture of something beautiful.
- Rearrange or tidy a small space.
- Work on a new project or craft (beading, cooking, origami).
- Doodle, paint, or color something just for fun.
- Try visual journaling by doodling or coloring freely.

- _____
- _____
- _____
- _____
- _____
- _____

Connection Joys
- Enjoy a fun activity with a loved one (play, day out, tea date).
- Call a friend who makes you laugh for a quick chat.
- Write a note of gratitude to someone on pretty stationery.
- Text someone: "Hey, just thinking of you—hope you're doing ok! :)"

- Do a small act of kindness.
- _____
- _____
- _____
- _____
- _____
- _____

A Spoonful of Joys (*culinary delights*)
- Eat your favorite meal for dinner.
- Bake a treat and take time to enjoy it during afternoon tea. Invite someone, and create a shared moment of connection and delight.
- Indulge in your favorite treat or snack slowly, noticing every flavor, texture, and aroma.
- Taste a fruit, snack, or spice you've never had before.
- Steep a warm cup of tea, and savor each sip mindfully.
- Try a new recipe for a hearty dish, and enjoy the process of creating something delicious.

- _____
- _____

- _____
- _____
- _____
- _____

Calm Joys
- Take a calm, relaxed stroll through the beauty of nature.
- Pause, steep, sip, and savor a cozy cup of tea.
- Do gentle stretches.
- Engage in intentional deep breathing.
- Wrap up in your favorite cozy blanket or wear warm socks.
- Step into a soothing shower—feel the water, breathe deeply, let go.
- Read a chapter of a book or listen to an audiobook.

- _____
- _____
- _____
- _____
- _____

- _____

Big Joys (*when you have more time*)
- Set off on an outdoor adventure to the beach, park, or beneath the open sky.
- Enjoy a feel-good movie that makes you smile.
- Dedicate time to a hobby.
- Embrace self-love and take yourself out (to a tea shop, bookstore, salon).
- Go for a jog or workout.
- Tidy and redecorate a corner or space in your home.
- Volunteer for a cause you care about.
- Light a candle, curl up on a comfy couch, turn on ambient sounds, and get lost in a good book with a warm drink.

- _____
- _____
- _____
- _____
- _____
- _____

Now, using your own Daily Habits of Joy Menu, personalize the next four weeks on the following pages by jotting down one small joy to look forward to each day, no matter how simple or fleeting it may seem. It can be a quick one-to-five-minute activity, a ten-minute pause, or, when time allows, hours of enjoyment. The goal is to deliberately create space for micro-joys on your calendar and honor them with the same care and respect you give your responsibilities.

By setting aside moments for small pleasures, you nurture your well-being and can invite more balance and happiness into your routine. Take time to thoughtfully mix and match the weekly calendars provided, blending them to craft beautiful monthly spreads that seamlessly fit into your planner or journal. Let it be a reminder that joy is not a luxury reserved for specific days or occasions, but rather, an essential part of every day and a fulfilled life. Let your small daily habits of joy be significant. Let them be enough. Let them lighten the weight of the day.

> ### SIP OF INSPIRATION
> Observe how small practices on your Daily Habits of Joy Calendar shape your week. Do you notice any positive shifts or more brighter days?

DAILY HABITS OF JOY
CALENDAR WEEK 1

MONDAY	TUESDAY
Try: Keep......... Swap.........	Try: Keep......... Swap.........
WEDNESDAY	**THURSDAY**
Try: Keep......... Swap.........	Try: Keep......... Swap.........
FRIDAY	**SATURDAY**
Try: Keep......... Swap.........	Try: Keep......... Swap.........
SUNDAY Try: Keep......... Swap.........	Which was most enjoyable or effective? Why?

DAILY HABITS OF JOY
CALENDAR WEEK 2

MONDAY	**TUESDAY**
Try: Keep_____ Swap_____	Try: Keep_____ Swap_____
WEDNESDAY	**THURSDAY**
Try: Keep_____ Swap_____	Try: Keep_____ Swap_____
FRIDAY	**SATURDAY**
Try: Keep_____ Swap_____	Try: Keep_____ Swap_____
SUNDAY Try: Keep_____ Swap_____	Which was most enjoyable or effective? Why?

DAILY HABITS OF JOY
CALENDAR WEEK 3

MONDAY	TUESDAY
Try: Keep......... Swap.........	Try: Keep......... Swap.........
WEDNESDAY	**THURSDAY**
Try: Keep......... Swap.........	Try: Keep......... Swap.........
FRIDAY	**SATURDAY**
Try: Keep......... Swap.........	Try: Keep......... Swap.........
SUNDAY	Which was most enjoyable or effective? Why?
Try: Keep......... Swap.........	

DAILY HABITS OF JOY CALENDAR WEEK 4

MONDAY	**TUESDAY**
Try: Keep_____ Swap_____	Try: Keep_____ Swap_____
WEDNESDAY	**THURSDAY**
Try: Keep_____ Swap_____	Try: Keep_____ Swap_____
FRIDAY	**SATURDAY**
Try: Keep_____ Swap_____	Try: Keep_____ Swap_____
SUNDAY Try: Keep_____ Swap_____	Which was most enjoyable or effective? Why?

18

Build a Life You Love

In San Francisco, it is a vibrant day of Spring under a calm blue sky. The hour is rather picturesque with flower petals raining, the sun shining brilliantly, and a feeling of endless possibility. The air is fresh and fragrant, the breeze cool and refreshing. We lay out a picnic, the blanket covered with hot food and sweet, cold fruits. Pouring tea from a thermos and relishing each sip, fully present, I feel every tension melt away. In this small moment, as I allow myself to truly experience this simple pleasure, I feel pure contentment and inspiration. It is this moment of serenity—made possible by a free and joyful mindset—that encourages my purpose.

I wish to inspire people to find and create more moments of beauty and joy in their everyday lives. With a passion for tea and a background in business and writing, I marry my purpose and my work, helping people create a life they love—one infused with tea, love, and gratitude. Through books, blogs, and much more, everything I do in my personal and professional life is fueled by my purpose and my mission to make the world a happier place—one positive thought at a time.

Years have passed in this pursuit, and now, as a mom, I continue to chase this mission with my little ones by thoughtfully shaping their daily routine. I rather think that teaching my young children the importance of growing gratitude, self-love, and an appreciation for life's simpler pleasures is one of the most valuable gifts I can give to them.

I have enjoyed storytelling since I scribbled my first fairytale on the back of a drawing at the age of nine. I always wished to contribute something positive to the world. Every person has a story to tell, and sharing yours might impact someone in ways you never imagined.

In the grand scheme of things, I am nobody. I am nothing. Yet, we are all needed. We *need* to be needed. To be happy, we need to serve others and see that we are helping them live better lives. In the end, we all mean something to someone else. We are all *somebody* to someone.

——— ✦ ———

The path to discovering your purpose might often be seen as a monumental task, reserved for the great thinkers, leaders, philanthropists, and creatives of the world. We might even think of purpose as an abstract, almost unattainable concept—something that only a few special people seem to discover. But what if your purpose isn't something hidden away, waiting to be unearthed? What if your purpose is already embedded within you, shaped by your experiences, your passions, and the world around you?

Let us think about the things that matter to you and energize you. We can explore how to find your purpose—not as a grand epiphany but as a gentle discovery that unfolds like blooming tea quietly unfurling. Then, we can consider ways to feel inspired, focused, and aligned with your deeper purpose.

Before we begin, it is important to understand what purpose truly means. It is not simply a career goal, an objective, or a checklist of achievements. It is the deep sense of direction that guides your decisions, fuels your motivations, and influences how you interact with the world. The contribution you endeavor to make to your community, to society, and possibly to the world is your purpose. It could involve helping others, creating something meaningful, seeking personal growth, or contributing to a cause that matters to you. It might look different at various stages of your life, but it is always tied to what makes you feel connected to yourself and the world.

Rather than viewing purpose as something you have to discover in an all-or-nothing way, think of it as a compass. While a compass isn't an exact map, it provides direction, helping you navigate to your destination. You won't necessarily have all the answers right away, and that's perfectly ok. With the right mindset, you can begin moving toward a life that feels authentic and fulfilling.

GUIDED BY YOUR INNER LIGHT

What truly matters to you? Finding your true calling often begins with self-reflection. Start by thinking about your core values—the principles that guide your life. These are the beliefs that shape your decisions and give you a sense of fulfillment when they are aligned with your actions.

Ask yourself questions like:
- What do I care about deeply?
- What principles do I refuse to compromise on?
- What makes me feel truly alive?

Within your values lies the quiet architecture of your destiny. What you carry in your heart shapes the life you're meant to live. It is the lens through which you interpret your experiences and the actions you take. If you find yourself disconnected from your guiding principles, it may be harder to recognize your purpose. This is why getting clear on what matters most to you is crucial.

Turn your gaze inward, focusing on the many hearts you carry, and the many parts you play. You are worthy and valuable. Like the crescent moon in the starlit sky, you shine bright and emit your light upon those in your little world. You beautify at least one person's world just by being in it. Think about everything that you do for the people around you. You might be a great spouse, parent, child, relative, friend, or citizen. You are dear to the people in your life, no, to this *world*.

The smallest deed you do, and the kindest word you say, makes a difference in somebody's life. Picking up a toppled plant can save it from being destroyed. Throwing unwanted bread outside for birds gives them extra food they can take home for their babies. Taking a quicker shower can help conserve the Earth's precious resource, water.

You are leading a life of purpose every day. You are taking care of your family and friends. Making someone laugh, cooking dinner for your family, and taking care of a sick relative might seem like things that you are expected to do, but, for a moment, think about what people's lives would be like if you were not there to do these things. The people around you need you. You have a special purpose in their life.

What makes you feel alive? Passion is the kind of trance when time forgets itself, where your hard work becomes a reflection of your joy, and you cannot help but offer it to others, like a gift from the heart. It is the sense of ease and fulfillment you feel when you're lost in an activity that comes naturally to you. Identify your top two passions. Devote a weekend to exploring each of these activities in-depth. Set aside other tasks and focus entirely on each area of interest.

Keep a journal to reflect on your feelings and experiences. Notice if time flies when you are engaged in a particular activity. Is there one you could imagine doing for years to come? This exercise will help you uncover your greatest passion.

LISTENING TO YOUR HEART'S COMPASS

Take notice of what brings you joy and flow, for purpose often reveals itself through the activities and moments that energize you and make you feel fully present. These are the things that give you joy without an external reward. They are the activities during which hours vanish unnoticed, and you gladly lose yourself in the experience.

Think about:
- When do I feel most alive and engaged?
- What activities make me forget the passage of time?
- What do I do that brings me a deep sense of satisfaction, regardless of the outcome?

When you're fully immersed in something you enjoy, it can be a significant clue to finding your purpose. Whether it's writing, helping others, creating, teaching, or problem-solving, these moments can serve as a guide to your true path.

Your life story is a rich source of insight into your purpose. Follow the ripples that linger and resurface in your tale. Reflect on key experiences, both big and small, that have shaped you into the wonderful person you are today. Pay attention to recurring themes, interests, and any patterns throughout your life. Have you consistently gravitated toward certain interests or causes? Have you found yourself in situations where you felt particularly alive or fulfilled?

Consider the following:
- What past experiences have shaped who I am?
- What themes or interests have emerged throughout my life?
- What have I learned from challenges or successes that could help me guide others?

While the answers might not be obvious at first, the patterns may be there. Perhaps you've been drawn to help others in various ways, or maybe you've always had a passion for creativity or problem-solving. Recognizing the recurring themes will give you a clearer understanding of what feels meaningful to you.

A deep commitment to your purpose can fill your heart with joy as you live a fulfilling, meaningful life. Hereupon, you may view the world through a more optimistic lens. With a clear vision and the ability to see the bigger picture, the trivial challenges that once caused you stress or frustration may lose their grip. You recognize your significance in this world and understand your worth. You respect yourself, knowing the positive impact your actions have on others. You feel valued when people acknowledge your contributions in both your home and in society. The sense of respect and satisfaction that you gain from this makes life even more precious, and you may feel compelled to care for your well-being.

WHERE YOUR PASSION MEETS YOUR PURPOSE

Think about how you can create value with your life, and how your presence can be a gift to those around you. Once you have discovered what you love to do, transform that passion into your purpose. Your talents can serve others and enrich their lives. Remember, your simplest acts can have the most profound impact. You don't need to be someone you're not, and you don't need to do anything extraordinary.

Every living being in this world has a purpose, no matter how small. Take a flower, for instance. It may only live for a short time, but in that time, it gives so much—its beauty, its scent, and its potential to give life to new flowers. In the same way, your life, too, has meaning, and through your actions, you will leave a lasting impression on the hearts of those around you.

Every living thing in this world is born with a purpose. Even the smallest flower gives so much. Let your thoughts drift to the red rose blooming graciously along bunches of shiny leaves. The rose is much more than a sight of beauty; it gives birth to new flowers. The rose emits a sweet scent into the atmosphere, a scent so divine that we emulate it with candles and perfumes. Depending on its fate, the rose will be picked and admired by a lovely person, or its time will slowly come to an end, and it will fall to the ground. Though as the rose says goodbye to all of the blossoms nearby, its withered petals will nourish the soil for new flowers that will bloom gracefully where it once did.

You are capable of doing great things, and everything you need to succeed is within you. You will make a difference in the lives of the many people in your world. Wherever you are, keep shining with the true happiness that is achieved through the habit of helping others.

19

Creating Room for Joy

On this cold, dark spring morning, the heater hums softly while I cradle a warm cup of tea with both hands. I listen to the rain and try to embrace the tranquility, but, to my surprise, my mind is brimming with thoughts and my heart with emotions. My body is slightly cold and slightly cozy from the plush golden-yellow sweater I am enveloped in. My mind—full of disarray and chaos—ponders the endless list of tasks on my calendar. My home sits untidy with things that I have accumulated over the years.

As a person of many passions and pursuits, I've lovingly collected countless items related to my hobbies and interests. Pretty ceramics, tea party decor, cute knick-knacks, and dusty souvenirs fill empty spaces, each item feeling like a small, silent weight in my life. The heaviness of physical clutter around me mirrors the emotional weight I carry. Unfinished tasks, scattered belongings, and unresolved feelings have created a sense of chaos, making it difficult to find peace. I soon learn that by decluttering my life in all areas—my home, my mental space, and my emotional world—I can create room for more joy, freedom, and happiness.

——— ✦ ———

It's not about perfection, but about intentional living through simplifying. Instead of striving for flawlessness and trying to make everything look perfect, our goal is to make room for what truly matters. It's about letting go of things that no longer serve you so that there is space to tap into a deeper sense of contentment and peace. Sometimes, in less, we find more meaning, and emotional freedom and happiness can have a chance to grow when we organize our lives. It's important to take time to tidy up your home, your mind, and your heart. Find beauty in simplicity, and embrace each day with intention.

TIDY CORNERS
QUIET THOUGHTS

Declutter your surroundings to create room for joy. Clearing your space is the first step toward a calmer, more intentional way of living. Begin by simplifying your immediate, physical environment—your home. Look around and identify objects that once fulfilled a purpose but are no longer needed or used. Things that become a source of stress rather than comfort should be cleared out. Take your time and gradually declutter your space, section by section.

When deciding whether to keep or donate an item, ask yourself whether it still adds value to your life. Does it make you happy? Does it bring you comfort? Does it fulfill a need? This isn't about throwing away things that are old or unwanted; rather, it is about letting go of things that are no longer necessary. You may continue this process until you feel lighter; it could take days or even weeks, and that is ok.

Oftentimes, removing physical clutter can also remove the mental burden of managing so many things. Letting go of items can feel like a small release of tension you are carrying. Carry on clearing away until your home starts to feel more peaceful and welcoming. It should be a space that nurtures you and allows you to breathe—a place you can relax without feeling stressed or anxious.

ONLY KEEP THE JOY

Unburden your thoughts. Once your physical space feels lighter, it's important to clear mental clutter, too. Sometimes, the clutter in our home reflects the chaos in our minds. Are your thoughts ever scattered? Are you dwelling on a to-do list that never seems to end? Are your thoughts filled with worries about the future? Are you holding on to regrets about the past? If any of those questions resonated with you, then a mental reset might be helpful. Just as it is important to declutter your surroundings to create space for peace, it is important to free your mind for the purpose of making room for positive thoughts and peace. Excessive inner noise can make it difficult to focus on the good things in life, feel gratitude, and be present.

Simplify your thoughts with a daily mindfulness practice. Each morning, set aside a few minutes to clear your head. Breathe deeply while focusing on the present moment. Quiet all the mental noise during this practice. Excuse the thoughts that interrupt the stillness. Focus on your breath. Spending a few moments on presence and awareness at the start of each day can help you feel less overwhelmed and more centered.

Journaling is another great way to declutter your mind. When you write down your thoughts and feelings, you are freeing up room for clarity and understanding.

Journaling is another great way to declutter your mind. When you write down your thoughts and feelings, you create space for clarity and understanding. Journaling can also help release worries and unhelpful thoughts. Write down and reflect on what affects you, and identify what truly matters so you can prioritize what deserves more of your attention and energy. Continue this process every day until you can calm your mind and set aside space for the most important things.

A LIGHTER LIFE BEGINS HERE

Lighten your heart's load. Freeing your heart from emotional baggage may be the most transformative part of your decluttering and simplifying journey. Now is the time to let go of emotions that no longer warm your heart. Those old grudges, unhealed wounds, and lingering resentments can weigh you down, and you should not make them valuable enough to store in your dear heart.

Forgiveness is a powerful way to liberate yourself and free your heart. Begin by forgiving yourself for past mistakes and then offer forgiveness to others who have hurt you. You don't have to maintain ties with the people involved, but conquer the power of the pain they caused you by forgiving them.

When you practice the act of forgiveness, you are not justifying disagreeable behavior, but rather, you are freeing yourself from the emotional grip it has on you. It's about lightening the load carried by your heart. By letting go of any regret, anger, or bitterness you may be holding onto, you carve out space for positive emotions such as acceptance, peace, and love.

Practicing gratitude is another wonderful way to let go of emotional clutter. Focus on the things you are thankful for—your health, your caring relationships, and the tiny treasures in life. By clearing away the emotional clutter of negativity, you can shift your emotional energy toward positivity. This process can help you simplify your life and cultivate more love and joy in your heart.

Seek splendor and serenity in simplicity. Releasing clutter from your home, your mind, and your heart can create a major shift in your life. You are creating space for joy every time you clear away things that no longer benefit you. Whether you let go of physical possessions, mental distractions, or emotional baggage, decluttering helps you open the door to fresh, new opportunities for peace and happiness.

A sense of openness and possibility may greet you in your newly decluttered home. The space can feel more soothing. There is room to relax, room to breathe, and a chance to focus on what truly matters, such as nurturing yourself, spending time with loved ones, and enjoying pleasant pastimes.

With mental clarity, you may discover that you have more time and motivation to pursue things you enjoy. The noise has quieted. Distractions have reduced. You might have more energy to nurture relationships. Feeling calm and emotionally present might inspire you to explore a new hobby, build upon your skills, or spend quality time with loved ones. You have created space in your mind and heart to enjoy the little things you may have previously overlooked.

Live life with intention. Decluttering and simplifying your home, mind, and heart can help you get rid of unfavorable things, thoughts, and feelings, and focus on enriching your life. Your journey of letting go may encourage you to shift your focus toward the important things in life—the people and pursuits that make you happy.

Tidying up your life is not just about discarding physical items; it's about making space for beautiful, uplifting things that deserve a place in your heart and mind. By doing this, you not only feel freer, but you are also able to be more intentional with your time and energy. You can determine which investments are worth making, whether emotional or of time. It's about dedicating your mind and heart to the lovely things that bring the light of beauty and the lift of joy to your everyday life.

What truly makes you happy? What gives you a sense of fulfillment? Instead of filling your life with things you don't need, activities that don't uplift you, or relationships that are draining, start focusing on what brings you peace, happiness, and purpose. Make fewer commitments and focus on meaningful activities. Achieve greater emotional freedom by cherishing supportive relationships. Curate your circle of friends, ensuring that the number of people you welcome into your personal world is small but special. Choose to spend time with people who align with your values and raise you, building strong and enriching relationships.

Having this intentional approach to life can help you gain greater calm and joy. Remember the power of letting go. Practice mindfulness. Experience the beauty of living in simplicity. Create room for what enriches your life and spirit.

20

Is There a Place Where Joy Grows Wild?

Joy unfolds when you shift your mindset. Powerful and life-changing, gratitude transforms our outlook on life and guides us toward a path of beauty and abundance. When we embrace gratitude and make it a part of our daily routine, we gently move our focus away from what's not good enough or what's missing. Instead, we choose to see the world in a softer, warmer light—one that illuminates the beauty that already exists.

Rather than dwelling on that which you don't have, cultivate a tiny habit of focusing on the abundance in your life and the joy that it already brings. By truly embracing simple yet profound gratitude practices in your everyday life, you can cultivate a mindset that invites a deeper sense of contentment. Focus on what's there, speak about what you have, and appreciate the people who are already present.

A GENTLE BLOSSOM: FROM THIRST TO RICHNESS

Through gratefulness, you can learn to turn your focus to the fullness of life. Instead of thinking about what you don't have or what could be better, regularly remind yourself about the wealth of goodness in your life. Think about the loveliness and the gentle joys that are flourishing in your life today. Make gratitude a part of your day by noticing and acknowledging the comforts and everyday treasures that enhance your daily life.

Practice speaking in the language of abundance. Since the language you use shapes your mindset, choose to speak from a place of plentifulness and possibility. Instead of saying things like "I don't have enough," or "I just wish I could," or "I will never be able to," speak with hope and appreciation. When you shift your language to focus on gratitude, you may say things like "I have what I need," and "I'm grateful for what I have." In addition to this, you may say, "I believe I can," and even "I attract opportunities," reinforcing bright feelings of plenty and promise.

> **SIP OF INSPIRATION**
>
> Every time you catch yourself saying, "I don't have this," try to replace it with, "But, I have this," reminding yourself about a specific blessing.

Shift your internal narrative for a big impact on your overall sense of gratitude. Practice speaking about what's already present in your life instead of dwelling on what's missing. Rather than focusing on what you lack, redirect your thoughts toward your potential. Everything you need is already within you. Your capabilities are waiting.

Did you know you can unlock a life of beauty and richness simply by embracing gratitude? Open your eyes to the gifts that surround you instead of focusing on gaps. A wealth of beauty and opportunities for growth and happiness are present in your life; shifting your mindset can inspire you to notice. You can bring positive changes to your life by infusing your daily routine with impactful gratitude practices. Beginning your morning with appreciation, writing in a journal, having gratitude teatime, expressing thanks to others, and savoring the little things can all brighten your outlook on life.

TO THE HEARTS THAT WATER MY HEART'S GARDEN

The generous love and support that you receive from your family and friends is a blessing. With grateful regard, thank them for their kindness. In a busy world where you may not always have time to connect with others in person, taking time to let people know that you value them is a tiny habit that can nurture relationships and deepen bonds.

Whether it's a family member, friend, significant other, or coworker, it's important to say "thank you" to make the other person feel appreciated. Perchance, they made you smile, gave you support, offered you kindness, or were simply there for you when you needed them. Acknowledge their positive impact on your life. There may be people in your life who make your world better just by being in it. Their presence is precious, and you should express gratitude for it.

Instead of waiting for birthdays or special occasions, make it a habit to regularly tell people you appreciate them. A seemingly small act with profound effects, expressing gratitude to others can take many forms, such as writing a thoughtful note, giving flowers, or sending a warm text message.

Putting in the effort to write a note to a friend who was there for you or taking a moment to thank your coworkers for their generous support can reinforce your connection. Feeling appreciated can uplift everyone's mood. Cooking a meal or baking treats to take to a family member to show them you care can brighten their day as well as your own. Expressing gratitude to your partner for their patience and affection can boost the love and good energy that flows between you, deepening your relationship.

Gratitude involves choosing to see your world in a softer, warmer light. Focus on daily gifts and moments that matter, be appreciative, and say thanks to the people who make life more beautiful. This gentle habit can help keep the positive energy flowing between you and your loved ones, boosting your sense of joy and well-being.

In every moment we meet with gratitude, there is beauty and potential for joy. Let us cherish the simple pleasures we have the luxury of indulging in each day. Let us honor and celebrate ourselves with kindness. Let us appreciate the spontaneous moments of blissful laughter we share with the people who make our heart's garden bloom. When we withdraw our attention from what is missing to what is already here, true happiness secretly unfolds, not as something we chase, but as something we *choose* to see, as something we *try* to feel.

"Joy grows wild in gardens of gratitude."

✦✦✦

21

When Joy Feels Far Away

There are sunny days, a great many, fragrant with blooming roses under bright, blue skies. Then there are days, gloomy and rainy, that suddenly wash away everything around you. Remember to look out for the rainbow, as darkness is not everlasting. Before long, the sun will shine again and brighten your day. Find comfort in the little things that warm your heart when the world is gloomy and cold. Seek beauty during times in which beauty is more difficult to see, for it may be in disguise, but it is there, waiting for you to hug it tightly.

When we open our hearts to gratitude, we can transform life's challenges into stepping stones, lightening our path and making the journey more beautiful. It may be easier to feel grateful when your day is bright with sunshine. But what about those cold, melancholy days, cloudy with despair? Strengthen gratitude during times of difficulty, for this is when it may have the greatest impact on your well-being. A strong mindset, rooted in appreciation for the good things, can inspire you to look for silver linings even in the darkest clouds.

A GRATEFUL HEART, A STRONG SPIRIT

Practicing gratitude during difficult times can transform your perspective on life. Turn your attention away from the difficult feelings you are experiencing in a tough situation by looking for lessons or opportunities for growth that they potentially present.

Encourage yourself to search for something to be grateful for in challenging situations. Take a moment to pause, search for even a flicker of positivity, and ask yourself: What is one wonderful blessing I have that has not been changed? What can I be grateful for today? Will I learn something from this that will ultimately empower me or make me stronger? While it may be harder to see the bright side during tough times, know that there is always something to learn or gain. Learning experiences, growth opportunities, kindness, beauty, or unexpected blessings may be hidden in moments of hardship.

By reframing difficult experiences, we can open ourselves up to the wisdom they offer. Whether it's an unpleasant incident in your personal life or a project at work that doesn't go as planned, acknowledge that every experience is a part of the journey. Gratitude empowers you to face difficult situations with acceptance and a sense of inner peace, making it a little easier to cope and move forward. It helps you realize that every challenge is a chance to learn something new and grow in ways you never imagined.

Reflect on how the experience could benefit you, focusing on the lessons it offers and the growth it can inspire. Will you learn a skill, develop a new interest, boost your confidence, or build resilience? Could you gain something beneficial? Or lose something that no longer serves you? Although it may not be easy to see at first, difficult situations—however troubling they may be—can have a positive side. Hold onto gratefulness tightly, and try to find something favorable, hidden in the smallest details, that will ultimately enrich your life.

Focusing on something positive or uplifting can also be helpful during tough times. Spending time on a hobby, volunteering for a cause that resonates with you, caring for a pet, and tending to the garden are just a few wonderful ways to keep busy. Try something that makes your heart lighter.

> **SIP OF INSPIRATION**
> Think about a new activity or hobby you would like to pursue as a way to find comfort during a difficult season. Is there something you want to learn or try?

HOLDING ONTO JOY, EVEN ON HARD DAYS

During difficult times, remember to count your blessings and embrace the small moments that make each day a gift. Spend more time in nature during the low points in life. Let yourself be enchanted by the beauty and grandeur of a moment in nature—the warmth of sunlight on your skin, the gentle breeze that kisses your face, and the fresh air that refreshes your spirit. Immerse yourself in life's simple pleasures to keep gratitude and positivity blossoming during moments of challenge. Be more present by engaging your senses with mindfulness and appreciation of the beauty around you.

Nature, even on the most difficult days, remains a vision of loveliness, bathed in soft light, alive with vibrant flowers. I walk beneath the towering Redwood trees, amid a plethora of plants that bedeck the verdant forest. These trees have been here for so long and have lived through so much, just like we will. Although they cast shadows and mystery, the forest is lit from above by the sun, with rays of light readily dancing through trees. Lush green leaves unfurl in dense, vibrant clusters, creating a scene so magically picturesque it almost feels like a dream. Trilliums, lupine, leopard lilies, and rhododendrons nestled among a sea of foliage and dewy grass sway blissfully.

Softening the landscape is a serene mist, calmly travelling through the forest, like a gossamer veil, evoking a sense of mystery and ethereal beauty. This is but one small part of the world, waiting for us to move forward toward the beauty and magic that awaits. Be open to finding a tranquil place beneath the sun and sky to enjoy quiet rumination. In nature's soothing embrace, you might find the inspiration you need to discover something to be grateful for during challenging times.

Just a quick look outside can often pacify the heart, too. The splendor that surrounds us can provide a gentle pick-me-up. No matter where we are or what we are doing, it can be helpful to pause and allow ourselves a moment to look out the window and notice something beautiful. The distant sky, the drifting clouds, and the dancing trees—steady things that say: the world is still here, still the same, and still holding you.

There's a quiet comfort in simply gazing outside and noticing the beauty that persists and the peace that remains. It can be calming and grounding. The morning air of the neighborhood you call home, the walls that hold your secrets, the gardens that see your joy, the breeze that whispers your stories—they are the same as before.

You are doing better than you think. You are amazing, and your life will become deepened after this temporary phase passes. Free your mind, filling it with appreciation and positivity, because you, my friend, will get through this.

> "When you wake up in the morning,
> plan to be happy, reminding yourself about
> one good reason to smile."

✦✦✦

22

Tea Parties and Tickle Fights

When you laugh, a wondrous joy lights up your face as laughter consumes you. When you play, your bright eyes twinkle, as though you are in love with life. When you have fun, the excitement wakes up your soul. You have the opportunity to laugh through your days. Nourish your body with food, your heart with love, and your soul with fun. When you enjoy yourself, you remember what you once knew so well at the age of five. The best part of life is playing and having fun.

Play is the language of childhood, but it should be an important part of our lives when we grow up, too. Research suggests that play can have numerous benefits for adults' physical and mental health. It can help reduce stress, increase physical activity, and improve our mood and outlook.

The magic of play lies in how it frees the spirit and positively affects our bodies. It is when we are fully present and absorbed in the moment. Our hearts, unguarded, are open to fully experiencing the emotions and sensations of our bodies moving ecstatically. Our minds have permission to wander, without reservation, constraints, or societal expectations.

We are unburdened, our hearts and souls untouched by restraint. Play becomes therapeutic. It's an act of self-care, a commitment to self-love. When we play, we, with unwavering heart, embrace the belief that we are enough, just as we are, and we deserve to be happy. We illuminate a profound truth: much contentment can be found if you allow yourself the freedom just to *be*.

There are many brilliant ways to incorporate more playfulness into your daily life. Play in adulthood can look different for everyone. It can be as simple as working on a puzzle, relaxing with a coloring book, and bouncing a ball. Trying a new board game, participating in a sport, creating art, playing cards, or sharing jokes with friends are great options as well.

Full of responsibilities, work, and daily demands, life can be quite tiring and stressful at times. Laughing and having fun are essential to restoring balance and joy. A profoundly necessary indulgence, play helps you take a step back from your day-to-day obligations and nourish your soul. It inspires you to do something enjoyable just for the sheer joy of it. There are no requirements, no time constraints, and no expectations. There is no pressure about getting it done correctly or on time.

Play is a celebration of the fun and amusement that persists in the world regardless of what goes on around you. It's a reminder that no matter what you have on your calendar, there's still much cheer, glee, and excitement in life, and you are meant to revel in it to lighten your load. Play can be anything you like to do recreationally that makes you happy. It is a special time to break free from the rigid structures of adulthood and follow your heart. Find fun activities that bring you pleasure and joy. It could be any experience that takes away stress, relaxes you, and envelops you, so time slips by unnoticed.

PLAYFUL THINGS YOU FORGOT YOU LOVED

- Board games
- Taking silly selfies to send to others
- Playing sports outside
- Playing games in an arcade
- Enjoying a carnival

- Blowing bubbles
- Flying a kite
- Coloring
- Counting the stars at night
- Dancing around the house
- Card games
- Going to an amusement park
- Drawing with chalk
- Eating ice cream
- Hula hooping
- Imaginative play
- Learning jokes to share with others
- Playing a video game
- Collecting stamps or stickers
- Playing with modeling clay or Play-Doh
- Writing or illustrating short stories
- Enjoying a train set
- Painting
- Playing games outside
- Running through sprinklers on a hot day
- Decorating
- Drawing
- Wearing something playful, like fun socks
- Jump rope
- Tea parties

- Making pottery
- Making jewelry
- Dance class
- Swimming
- Engaging with exhibits at the zoo
- Gardening
- Tickle fights
- Parks
- Jumping in puddles after a rainstorm
- Playing mini golf
- Journaling
- Collecting sea shells or unique leaves
- Miniature polymer clay creations
- Scrapbooking
- Water balloon fight
- Collecting and pressing flowers or leaves

We will always need little ways to feel more at ease. Write a list of things to do just for the fun of it, and find ways to add them to your calendar. It could be anything you love that sparks creativity, inspires you to be more active, or aids in managing stress more effectively.

Spending all our time on productive activities can leave us feeling empty. When life feels draining, energize your spirit with good old fun. Try something relaxing and carefree for no reason but joy. Permit yourself to enjoy life's lighthearted pleasures more often. You might play Connect Four with a family member, become absorbed in hours of crafting, practice a new dance, or solve a puzzle. Every cheerful experience that you have embellishes the tapestry of your life.

Play belongs to everyone. It is not just for the young. Every weary soul can benefit from this humble human experience. Every journey can be enriched with the colors of playfulness. It is essential for a balanced and fulfilling life.

Develop a playful approach to life. Think of ways to make everyday activities more fun.

TINY ACTS OF PLAY

Instead of journaling to reduce stress, you might try a coloring book for a change.

Instead of swimming laps, you might have a swimming contest with your children or friends.

Instead of sitting on the beach, you might play volleyball or build a sand castle.

Instead of going to the gym, try a dance class.

Instead of watching tv, you might go outside, lie on the grass, and watch the clouds, birds, trees, and nature.

Instead of calling a friend to catch up, you can draw or paint a card and mail it to your friend.

Instead of buying a gift for someone, you might make them jewelry, soap, candy, or a beautiful craft.

Instead of going shopping, you might go to a carnival.

Instead of listening to music, you might try to play an instrument or sing your own song.

Instead of spending an hour on social media, write or illustrate a short story or poem.

The power of play is undeniable. As adults, we often forget the magic and joy of play and rarely make time for it amid our busy schedules. By prioritizing and adding it to your routine, you can bring more of it into your life. Encourage your inner child to lead the way, giving yourself the privilege of being engrossed in play. Watch your life blossom through fun, joyful activities that encourage happiness and merry spirits.

Connect with others through play, and share a playful experience. In the late afternoon, the sunlit houses illuminate the neighborhood like tall candles, gently lighting our lives as the sun gets ready to set and the moon prepares to show its handsome face. Children glide along on their scooters—a boy in black shorts, a girl in a white dress. Their mother rushes behind them. The kids' squeals give this scene a familiar name—fun.

RECLAIM THE JOY OF PLAY

It is in the warmth of playful amusement that one can often find oneself beaming with a heart full of contentment and eyes filled with sparkling joy. To feel this marvelous sensation, one must take time to have more fair-weather adventures. Eat out of a picnic basket, sleep under the stars, have a diverse dinner party, enjoy a carnival, and spend an hour in whimsy. When this is not enough to soothe your soul, splurge on ice cream or hot chocolate. Seek opportunities for joyful entertainment. We must set out on a new playful adventure every month to ensure that we are living life to the fullest. Celebrate holidays, and join a fun club so you can have an escapade to look forward to regularly.

Have a picnic. Frolicking in the park with kids or pets is a most agreeable way to spend a day beneath the beautiful blue skies. You might entertain the idea of going to a scenic park with plenty of space to eat and play. Invite as many family members as you can to maximize the fun.

Enjoy a beautiful day under the sun with family, food, and fun. Eat cold sandwiches from a basket and sip fruit juice from a box. Fly a kite, throw a frisbee, or play a game. Soccer, volleyball, freeze tag, and capture the flag are a few possibilities to consider. If there are swings in the park, hop on and see how high you can go!

Take a camping trip. Leave all your niceties behind and enjoy a day full of happiness in nature. Don't forget to pack hot cocoa and plenty of marshmallows. They will make a yummy treat when you are stargazing. Consider taking a captivating book so you can share stories by the campfire. If spending a night out at a campsite gives you the collywobbles, then perhaps you might camp out in your living room or backyard instead. Feel the warmth of the day transform into a zephyr exclusive to a spring night. Watch as the world—an amusement park—gently comes to a close, and those who have indulged in its gifts are going to bed with full hearts.

Have a diverse dinner party. Plan a feast with food, drink, and dessert from a different culture. Rather than opting for the popular dishes you are familiar with, find recipes for foods that are highly sought after in their respective countries. If you wish, you can get some snacks and desserts from a nearby restaurant. However, the goal is to learn how to cook an unfamiliar dish. Expose yourself to other cultures. Go to ethnic grocery stores to obtain ingredients you need. Don't hesitate to try new things, as doing so opens the door to a vibrant, spicy, and adventurous lifestyle.

When was the last time you went to a festival or a fair? Reconnect with the child within you who still seeks adventure, wonder, and cheer. Let the whimsical melody of the merry-go-round envelop your ears, for this is the sound of childhood, innocence, and carefree joy. Become entranced by this fanciful land. Sink your teeth into a cherry-flavored snow cone. Hold a pink cotton candy cloud in your hand, and let fluffs of it melt into sweetness on your tongue. Play a game of ring toss, and try to win a giant, cuddly teddy bear. Open your heart to the magic, the gaiety, the wonder.

Have a tea party. Set a charming, refined tea table in your garden, evoking timeless elegance. Drape pretty, lace linens over the table. Delicate, paper doilies can adorn each place setting. Set out a beautiful tea set that delights you. From gorgeous vintage pieces to elegant heirlooms or modern designs, whatever you choose will be the jewel of your tea party. Mix and match delicate cups and saucers to heighten the whimsy and charm of your affair. Prepare dainty desserts that look too good to eat, and make a selection of petite sandwiches.

Hang bunting, colorful lanterns, or pom-poms from tree branches or above the table. Gather a bright assortment of fresh flowers and arrange them in a pretty teapot so that it can serve as a tasteful centerpiece for your table. Invite a few of your favorite people over for tea. You could serve yummy scones, sandwiches, and treats for a quintessential afternoon tea. Have a cheerful gathering, for it is moments like these that you and your guests will cherish.

Organize a playful ice cream treat party. One summer's day, invite family and friends to celebrate the sweetness of life. Connect over creamy scoopfuls of joy made with a simple yet heavenly combination of milk and sugar. Use colorful ice cream cups as a fun alternative to cones. Think about whether you want candy, sprinkles, and sugary toppings, or a delicious selection of nutritious offerings like fresh fruit and granola. Use ice cream parlor-inspired decorations, and send out cute invitations to get your guests excited about the party. Such a gathering can be scrumptious with ice cream, gelato, and frozen yogurt, too. Taste a spoonful of this and that. Smile at the spoon. It might smile back.

Throw a chocolatey get-together. Sip, chat, and cozy up with a cup of hot cocoa. Place fun, colorful mugs on a tray and fill them with this comforting drink to give your guests warmth and cheer. You can offer marshmallows, rolled wafer cookies, and other tasty toppings. A heaping swirl of whipped cream with sprinkles on top? Now *that's* a treat that would put anyone in a joyful mood.

For an extra touch of fun, consider setting up a hot cocoa bar with snacks. Munch on buttery popcorn or salty pretzels. Savor your hot cocoa while watching a movie that carries you on an exciting adventure or has you laughing until your stomach aches.

Experience playful entertaining. What do you do for fun during your parties? What kinds of games or activities do you plan for entertaining your guests? Do you watch television or engage in juicy conversations? Try something novel and exciting! How do makeovers and fashion shows sound? Exciting, right?

You can purchase makeup for everyone to share, or ask the guests to bring their own. Arrange a professional makeup artist if your budget allows this, or let the ladies give each other makeovers. The latter option is more interactive and fun! Make sure there are lots of sparkly hair accessories and jewelry. You can provide them, or ask everyone to come accessorized.

Once everyone is all glammed up, get a camera ready, and find a stage for the fashion show. You can lay out a red carpet or decorate a designated area to serve as the ramp. Play upbeat music that suits the glamorous moment. Let each person do her signature catwalk, and capture her exciting, glitzy, awkward, or silly moment in a picture or video that you can share with her. Your get-together is sure to be unforgettable!

Celebrate as many holidays as you can. Seasonal events, whether meaningful or utter nonsense, add something special to the air. Couples might put a little more effort into spoiling each other for Valentine's Day. On Mother's Day, we remember that our moms are the true queens of our hearts. The holidays are a rather magical time with glittering lights, tinsel-covered trees, and candy cane lanes.

Get in the holiday spirit! Wearing the colors that represent holidays and baking goodies to celebrate is good old fun. It can be an easy way to incorporate more playfulness into your life. You get to take a break from your mundane agenda and do something unique and amusing. Make up your own holiday so you can have fun stuff to look forward to year-round. You can have a spa day, an annual bake-off, or a day of biking through town. Dedicate a day to plants by hosting a garden party and planting a tree or a flower. Celebrate animals by adopting a vegetarian diet for a week or visiting a farm.

Join a club. If you want to add more play to your life regularly, you could join a community in which you can connect with others through exciting activities. Many clubs can help you boost physical activity, such as swimming, tennis, yoga, golf, basketball, or dancing. If you aren't able to find one that interests you, think about starting your own club. This can be as simple as inviting family, friends, or neighbors to join you for bowling, beading, playing an instrument, horseback riding, or biking.

You can also start your own club by inviting a group of people to go for a walk in the park once a week. You can meet with members from your book club during tea time a few times each month. You can have a movie night with your best friend once a month. Use play to brighten your days and treat yourself to the fullness of life.

Laughing with family and friends nurtures joyful moments of connection and warmth—memories we hold fondly through time. Strengthen your relationships and fortify bonds through laughter and play. Enjoy fun games, watch a comedy, or learn jokes to promote playfulness in relationships. Laugh at nonsense. It's required regularly. Sharing happiness with loved ones weaves beautiful, lasting memories we carry through life like treasures of the heart. Play allows us to hug the moments that fill our lives with true beauty—moments when we release our worries, laugh wholeheartedly, sing happily, dance freely, and simply exist.

> **SIP OF INSPIRATION**
>
> Describe something you like to do just for fun that makes you feel playful, free, or happy. Invite a loved one to join you for this activity.

Using the words below, try this word search puzzle to find a list of fun things to do.

Cookies Race Snowball Bounce Shower Rain
Games Adventure Trip Song

R	A	N	E	C	E	E	M	A	G
S	A	P	L	C	M	C	O	O	K
M	G	I	N	T	R	G	A	M	R
I	N	U	N	X	B	T	D	R	E
L	O	B	A	L	R	Z	P	H	W
B	S	S	E	I	K	O	O	C	O
L	O	M	P	S	H	O	W	F	H
A	G	A	M	E	S	Q	W	J	S
F	L	L	A	B	W	O	N	S	I
E	R	U	T	N	E	V	D	A	N

1. Sing in the _____ in a funny pitch.

2. Take a road _____ with no planned itinerary. Off you go!

3. Compose a silly _____ with a catchy chorus. Sing it to someone who could use a laugh.

4. Play board _____ with your family.

5. Have a _____ fight.

6. Bake _____ with kids and decorate it together.

7. Have a potato sack _____ in your backyard.

8. When it starts sprinkling, right before the _____ look up at the sky and feel the cold drops of water on your face.

9. When attending a kid's birthday party, take your shoes off, hop in the _____ house, and jump your socks off. Yippee!

10. On a random weekday morning, if possible, call in sick to work, and set out on an _____ in the city.

Never stop having adventures. You will laugh so hard your jaw will hurt, your cheeks will get sore, your eyes will tear up, and your stomach will ache, but don't skip these enjoyable discomforts, because this, *this* is the meaning of living life.

"Laughter is when your heart sings, and your soul does a happy dance."

✦✦✦

23

A Little Habit to Heal the Heart

Today is an opportunity to learn. Today is an opportunity to grow. On the journey toward flourishing, you might make mistakes, perhaps stumble, and maybe even fall. Despite this, you rise again, year after year, as a wiser, stronger, more whole version of yourself. It's time to truly forgive yourself for missteps, regrets, and anything else that may be holding you back from loving yourself unconditionally.

Forgiveness is a profound act. It carries the silent power to heal wounds, restore peace, and nurture personal growth. To forgive ourselves and others is to unlock a profound strength, loosen the grip of resentment and guilt, and open the door to healing, growth, and lasting joy.

HEALING WITH SELF-COMPASSION

As you walk the path of self-love and compassion, hand yourself the bouquet of forgiveness—an act of healing only you can give. We are all imperfect beings, and that is exactly how we are meant to be. We are prone to making mistakes, and sometimes, our errors come with consequences that leave us with feelings of guilt or unworthiness. Whatever happens, remember that your mistakes do not define who you are. Your errors do not lessen your worth. One misstep does not alter the course of your journey. Forgiving yourself means recognizing that you are human, that errors are an inevitable part of life, and that these mistakes can serve as valuable lessons.

Forgiving yourself is not about excusing poor choices or denying responsibility for actions. It's about acknowledging and also accepting what happened, and embracing the ability to grow from experiences. Holding onto guilt or self-blame hinders personal growth. Such negative emotions can gain control over a part of your life, preventing you from gaining valuable wisdom and moving forward. Self-forgiveness makes it possible to release the emotional weight of past actions and create space for self-compassion. It is a gentle process of allowing ourselves to heal, learn, and grow.

When you forgive yourself, you pave the way to cultivating self-worth, as it empowers you to see yourself not through the lens of past mistakes but through the eyes of someone worthy of love, respect, and kindness. When you choose to let go of the past and become free from regret, you open the door to new possibilities, joy, and a brighter future.

Whatever is holding you back, it is time to forgive yourself and move on. Take time to reflect on what happened and explore where things might have become disagreeable. Identify what you can learn, and how you can avoid repeating the same mistakes. Rather than dwelling on past errors, it's time to channel your energy toward personal growth, positive change, and future success. If necessary, sincerely apologize to yourself or those affected. Write about it, talk to someone about it, and get the closure you need to move forward. It is through forgiveness that we free ourselves, no longer letting the past dictate our present or future.

LETTING GO, FINDING PEACE

Embracing mercy for those who have hurt you is another important part of liberating yourself, as it can help you achieve emotional freedom. There is something beautifully transformative about letting go. Forgiveness carries the transformative power to heal broken trust, rebuild relationships, and restore peace. It can set you free from the pain someone has caused you. Requiring empathy, compassion, and the willingness to see beyond the hurt, extending grace to others can, with time, heal the heart.

When we are wronged, we may naturally hold onto feelings of anger, sadness, or resentment, letting them build up inside. Often, however, such emotions can become toxic if we let them simmer beneath the surface for too long. Carrying the burden of resentment toward others can cloud our judgment. It can increase negative thoughts and harm our relationships, preventing us from finding peace and joy.

Sometimes people may hurt others because of their own insecurities, pain, or problems. Viewing the situation with empathy can help us understand that their words or actions may not actually have been a direct reflection of who we are. Rather, their behavior could be coming from their own pain, internal struggles, and personal inadequacies. Still, it is never okay for you to have to hurt as a result of the shortcomings of another. Nevertheless, this shift in perspective might soften the heart, making forgiveness not only easier but also more meaningful.

It is difficult, but pardoning others to unburden our own hearts is beneficial for our own well-being. Forgiveness is an act of emotional liberation—a courageous reclaiming of our happiness and a gentle step toward lasting peace. This doesn't mean that we are condoning poor behavior or excusing the harmful actions that hurt us. Forgiving simply means choosing to release the power that the other person's negative actions have over us and reducing the pain. It allows us to release the emotional weight we carry, improving our sense of inner peace. Forgiving someone doesn't mean you keep them in your life. It is for you to determine if a person is truly worthy of a place in your heart, for even after releasing others with kindness, reconciliation is not always possible.

Determine the value and the goodness that the person contributes to your life. If you are uncertain, you might ask yourself some insightful questions and write the answers in your journal for reflection. Does this individual support your well-being? What mistake has the person made, and how likely are they to repeat it? Is this somebody who adds laughter and love to your life? Or is this person responsible for negativity, stress, and more grief than joy? If the person conflicts with your values or your goal for happiness, then fitting such a person into your life can ultimately cause more harm. In that case, a proper parting is overdue.

Your friends and companions should uplift you, making you feel at ease so you can shine as your authentic self. If someone makes you feel otherwise, then it may be time to forgive and move on in life, creating space for more nurturing friendships and relationships.

Your heart is like a little garden. The flowers you plant are like the friends you keep. You can plant lovely flowers that add beauty and fragrance to your life. Once in a while, you must take time to remove the weeds from your garden. Yes, weeds are still plants, just like people who hurt you are still people.

However, weeds negatively impact a garden by reducing the growth and productivity of desired plants. They can quickly deplete the soil of water and nutrients that your garden plants need to thrive. Weeds—or people who are not a good fit—can adversely affect your life and your heart's garden. The sooner you get rid of the weeds, either through forgiveness or a goodbye, the sooner your heart's garden can bloom again and flourish with peace and joy.

Forgiving yourself and others is one of the most important acts we can perform. It is liberating, allowing us to release the negative emotions that bring us pain. It is empowering, helping us to heal from past wounds. Letting go helps us create space for growth so that we can achieve our full potential. It is through forgiveness that transformation begins, a healing of the heart that leads us toward greater freedom, deeper compassion, and lasting emotional resilience.

24

Gratitude as Your Guide Through Hardships

In the dance of life, we rise and fall to the melody of bright dawns and shadowed dusks. Just as every rose bears its thorns, every joy, too, gets kissed by sorrow. But remember—every sorrow brings with it the seed of joy, waiting to be realized, waiting to enrich your life with beauty and fragrance.

Life, as we all know, can be unpredictable. One moment, everything seems to be going well, and the next, something distressful can occur out of nowhere, leaving us feeling lost or hopeless. Regardless of whether it's a personal challenge, a familial conflict, a loss, or a career setback, the pain that accompanies these struggles can be insufferable. However troubling they may be, there are ways to cope with life's challenges, and the healing power of gratitude can be incredibly helpful.

If you are experiencing stress, grief, heartache, or difficulty, gratitude can be an empowering tool for emotional recovery and strength. Embrace this gentle art of appreciation when times are good, and hold onto it with even greater perseverance during hard times. This simple yet profound habit has the potential to heal, to nurture growth, and to bring joy back into your life.

Gratitude is not merely the companion of good times, reserved for moments of success and happiness. Rather, it is a gentle light that flickers even in the midst of sorrow, waiting for you to discover it. Finding peace, strength, and positive lessons during difficult times is invaluable, and gratitude carries the glow that can brighten your journey.

Have you ever experienced an unpleasant time in your life when you felt completely lost, hopeless, upset, or heartbroken? Were you struggling to bear the weight of your emotions? It can be difficult to regain a sense of balance during such times. Finding peace and realigning with your purpose may feel difficult. Instead of being stuck in a state of sadness or disappointment, choose to reframe your thoughts to find healing and improve your state of being. In the midst of difficulty, search for something to be grateful for, gently shifting your attention away from the pain and toward positive or productive thoughts.

Studies show that practicing gratitude can help support emotional healing. While gratitude may not be able to change your circumstances, it can help change your perspective on them. Shift your mindset by focusing on the enduring blessings that bring you comfort and joy. Think about the little things you are thankful for that still embellish your life. Let your heart linger on life's simple pleasures, savoring them often as reminders that even now, light and joy find their way in. There are other opportunities to pursue. There are new adventures to be had. Gently reframe the way you see this moment, taking notice of not what is absent, but the overflowing beauty that exists in the here and now. Allow gratitude to guide you through pain, one breath at a time. And remember, every step forward is worth celebrating.

WHAT IF YOU ALREADY HAVE EVERYTHING YOU NEED?

Focusing on what we don't have can sometimes contribute to feelings of disappointment and pain. It can be easy to get caught in the mindset of "I lost" or "I don't have enough" of something. However, thinking about what's missing from your life can quickly start to feel overwhelming and stressful, whether it's an opportunity, a project, love, friendship, time, success, or support. Try to reduce the unpleasant emotions you experience as a result of focusing on what is lacking. Use gratitude to change the way you think about your circumstances in life. Instead of directing your attention to what's lacking, focus on what's there, waiting to be enjoyed. The more you notice, the more you will have.

Gratitude teaches you that what you already have is enough. You can make the life-changing shift from seeing what is absent in your life to celebrating what's already there. It can be difficult to see emptiness as wholeness. When going through a difficult time where you feel like you have lost something, consciously choose to focus on what you still have. Every day, think about the blessings that still bloom in your life today—your mind, your health, your family, your friends, your ability to smile, your capabilities, your strengths.

Be present to the lovely details around you, for the world is still as beautiful as it was before the distressful situation occurred. Maybe you stopped noticing the everyday beauty in your path, but it is still there, waiting for you to embrace it. Life can still be pleasant. With a grateful heart, think about the good people who are still in your life, giving you love, support, and thoughtful acts of kindness.

A GENTLE WAY THROUGH THE HARD THINGS

Gratitude isn't just about recognizing life's lovely blessings. You can also use it to process pain and let go of resentment. As you walk the path toward healing, it's important to find some peace amidst emotional turmoil. You don't have to ignore your feelings or bottle them up. Instead, let them fade softly into the past. Embrace gratitude to free yourself from the weight of those uncomfortable feelings.

If you find yourself walking through a painful time, open your heart and allow yourself to sit with your feelings of despair and hurt freely. As you reflect, acknowledge the pain, but, at the same time, think about a lesson this experience has taught you. Allow yourself to release bitterness and let go of the anger or sadness that weighs you down by focusing on a way the hardship has benefitted you—whether it strengthened you, made you wiser, or helped you grow. Forgive yourself and anyone involved, allowing peace to come as you release. Heal your heart with appreciation, for even the trials you face carry their own hidden blessings.

You can gain a bit of liberation from the pain of negative experiences by being thankful for the growth that you have experienced during times of difficulty. Acknowledge the strength you have built and the quiet ways your life has grown. Recognize the resilience you have discovered within yourself, and know that with this spirit, you can slowly move forward, having gained something positive. Revere the lessons you have learned, the skills that you have improved upon, or the support you have received that has strengthened other relationships in your life. This delicate and unhurried process of healing can help you release heavy feelings no longer needed on your journey. Through acceptance and peace, gratitude can empower you to take steps toward joy.

Adding simple practices of appreciation to the soothing routines of your daily life can have a profound impact on your path to blooming again. To help you stay grounded, you might begin each day with a grateful spirit, taking a moment to reflect on three good things in your life. Think about the pleasures that make your morning pleasant—such as the warmth of that first cup of tea or coffee, the peaceful sound of the birds chirping outside your window, or the comfort of having all your favorite things around you.

You are encouraged to set a positive intention for the day, such as "Today, I will think more positively by challenging negative thoughts with helpful ones," or "Today, I will be more grateful by reframing thoughts of scarcity with abundance that I am blessed with." This can help set an optimistic tone for the day ahead. Empowering self-love affirmations and gentle reminders can also be uplifting during times of difficulty. Try incorporating any of these promising practices into your morning routine to help you feel more emotionally balanced.

If journaling helps you feel better, spend a few minutes reflecting on the blessings that remain. It can be the smallest joys hidden in ordinary moments, and the little treasures that brighten your day. The more time you spend on appreciating what you have, the less you will waste on thinking about what you lost. Lift your spirits with gratitude tea time in the afternoon. Soothe your soul by being present and mindful during a walk outside. Warm your heart and that of others by saying thanks to supportive family and friends.

Hold close the gratitude habits that help you feel calm and as if your emotions are beginning to settle. Is there a particular practice that makes you feel more grounded and resilient, strengthening your heart and offering hope for each day? Even in the darkest of times, there is something to be grateful for if you encourage yourself to feel beyond the hurt. Try to look beyond the hardship.

See the beauty around you—still glorifying your part of the world. The magic, the wonder, the love, the happiness—it all waits for your warm embrace. Don't deny yourself joy today over something that happened yesterday. Today is an opportunity to laugh. Today is an opportunity to grow. Let yourself experience the heartwarming gifts of life that grace your path today.

CELEBRATE PERSONAL GROWTH

In the tender act of healing from adversity, one may stumble upon a discovery—one of profound beauty, one of personal growth. It is the gentle blooming of the self, developed by enduring pain and embracing gratitude. One may discover hidden talent, newfound strength, and previously unknown resilience. Open your heart to the joy of personal growth born from sorrow.

It is in times of difficulty that the opportunity for enrichment may quietly present itself. Growing through gratitude can be an enlightening process of self-discovery, empowerment, and improvement. Through the art of appreciation, you learn to see that the obstacles you face are not setbacks, but rather, stepping stones that shape you into the amazing person you are becoming. During the challenging time, did you discover something about yourself, learn a new skill, grow, or rediscover your own rhythm? This is all a beautiful part of personal growth, and achieving such awareness is, in itself, worthy of celebration. The path to healing is not always straightforward. It is filled with both pain and progress, forming a delicate balance that helps you bloom into a more radiant and resilient version of your authentic self.

> **SIP OF INSPIRATION**
> Think about a challenge you've faced. How has the experience helped you grow? Celebrate one way you've become wiser, stronger, or more resilient.

Be appreciative of your growth, acknowledging that you are constantly evolving, learning, and adapting. Experiences that challenge you can help you gain new wisdom and insight into who you are and what matters most to you.

Healing after hardship isn't about returning to the way things were, but about becoming stronger, wiser, and more connected to yourself. The heart's recovery can be an intricate process—one that takes time, patience, and intention. Take it one day at a time, with each day made brighter through gratitude practices, and you may find it easier to move forward with peace and strength. Focus on the beauty, blessings, lessons, and growth that come with every sunrise.

While gratitude asks you to appreciate the good things, it is not exclusively for the good times. Rather, it means consistently acknowledging life's sweetness and abundance, even when light feels far away. Gratitude, you may soon discover, has the power to transform the way you see the world and live your life. It can improve your relationship with not just your circumstances, but also with yourself.

25

A Daily Cup of Kindness, Warm and Sweet

Let us be the pouring rain after long hot days of summer. Let us be a radiant rainbow on a day dimmed by showers. Let us be the sunrise that illuminates the new beginning of the day. Let us be light where darkness dwells. In the end, the story we leave behind does not boast our achievements or our wealth. Rather, it speaks of the kindness we have shown—the hearts touched, the minds inspired, the spirits lifted, and the moments made brighter through our presence. Let us then choose kindness—not as a planned act that we perform every so often, but as a way of life, as a light we carry into every room, as our way of making the world a better place.

Kindness is a small yet mighty act that is capable of changing lives, communities, and the world. Within our busy lives, our schedules may have little to no space for benevolence. We may forget the power of small, kind gestures. There are many ways to cultivate a tiny habit of kindness in your daily routine. A sincere compliment, a note of encouragement left for a stranger, or a moment of listening can be a lantern for someone lost in fog.

One doesn't need to have a lot of money, time, or resources to live a life flourishing with kindness. It is about embracing a mindset that prioritizes empathy, respect, and compassion in our everyday interactions. It's not all about doing good deeds. Practicing kindness in daily life means nurturing a positive environment that encourages compassion, connection, and harmony. Kindness asks us to soften the gaze through which we view others, seeing not only their actions but also the unseen hardships they face and the burdens they silently carry. We can do our part in creating a more harmonious world by meeting others with empathy rather than judgment, with an open heart rather than indifference, and with patience rather than irritation.

A little kindness goes a long way, especially to yourself. This journey begins with you, and you must not forget the gentleness owed to the self through self-compassion and positivity. When you are kind to yourself, you plant a seed from which your generosity toward others can grow. Always remember that your heart is a little garden. Nurture beauty within through words of warmth and tenderness, offering your heart a safe and nurturing space to heal and grow.

Forgive yourself for past mistakes, embrace the lessons you have learned, and the person you have grown into. If you catch yourself questioning your abilities, recall your self-worth and celebrate who you are. Hold yourself in loving kindness. Treat your mind and body with care every day through rest and a nourishing self-care routine. As you become gentler with yourself, extending kindness to others can come more naturally. A heart well-tended may find it easier to gift the empathy and generosity it too enjoys. Nurture your inner sanctuary so that love may overflow, ever more abundant, ever more radiant.

Through kindness, we graciously sow seeds that will blossom in gardens we may perhaps never see. With generosity, we water it. With patience, we prune it. In return, we aspire not to pick fruits or flowers of honor or praise, but peace and contentment of the soul. Making lives you encounter a little brighter, making the world a bit more beautiful and fragrant, is in itself fulfilling. So let us be the gardeners who tend first to our own hearts, and then, from a place where an abundance of love blooms, scatter seeds of benevolence wherever we go.

Invite beautiful musings of kindness to bloom quietly within you, like a flower kissed by morning light. Gentle and positive thoughts have a soft power to shift your gaze toward the good. Since your thoughts shape your feelings, it's important to remind yourself to think kindly. Should your reflections dwell on people, things, or experiences, perhaps you might gently replace any adverse thoughts with ones filled with empathy. Let compassion be the lens through which you see the world. Thinking negatively about others can hinder your ability to see the beauty around you fully. It can prevent you from truly finding happiness. In addition, it can deprive you of the friendship and joy that may come from certain people you may not think well of.

Unkind thoughts can harm your joyful mindset by creating negative, gloomy feelings that can dim your sunshine. View others with empathy, understanding that everyone is facing their own battle. Stress, problems, and the struggle for happiness are a part of everyone's life. Be considerate of others and understand that they may be going through difficult times. Try to avoid seeking flaws and forming judgments about people you come across.

Polluting your thoughts regarding others with unwarranted suspicion can conflict with thinking kind thoughts. Have neutral thoughts about people you meet, and let their words and actions define them. Choose to see the best in others rather than search for their flaws. Steep your thoughts in the gentle warmth of peace and positive light. Let us uplift ourselves by lifting others. See the world's inherent loveliness, and treat everyone with respect and fairness.

LET KINDNESS BE YOUR VOICE

Be mindful of how your words will affect others. Soften your voice, engage in a gentle conversation, give a kind compliment, or share a meaningful silence. To cultivate kindness, it's important to be thoughtful about the language we use. Our words are seeds that hold the power to grow thriving gardens or create deserts of despair. They have the ability to elevate others, to bring others down, to make others laugh, and to make others cry. Words can hurt. Words can heal. When speaking to yourself and others, choose words that are uplifting, thoughtful, and supportive.

Be generous with compliments, offer encouragement, and provide support when needed. Be aware of the way your words can impact the listener. Will it brighten their day? Will it hurt their feelings? Try to avoid words that are critical or negative. Aspire to be the source of positive, kind words in someone's life—we all need it.

Remember, your words have the power to heal the broken, soothe the exhausted, uplift the defeated. With gentle and inspiring words, we can create a more favorable environment in which everyone can enjoy a little more positivity and connection. In a world where people are led by their delicate hearts, words of kindness are the golden threads that can connect souls.

Speaking kindly about others is just as important as speaking kindly to others. We journey together in this deeply connected world. Indulging in gossip at work, in social circles, or among friends can be a tempting way to bond. Unfortunately, gossip has negative consequences for both the individual being talked about and the person spreading it. Thriving on judgment and possibly false gossip can turn a group's energy toxic.

Turn away from speaking unsavory words that mock your fellow beings or can harm their reputations. If your group's conversation is heavily focused on gossip, change the topic and encourage everyone to talk about good things. If you find yourself criticizing others or spreading rumors, pause, and remind yourself that this is not the way to a life of goodness and joy.

Shape a nurturing space where helpfulness, kindness, open-mindedness, and collaboration can flourish. Steering clear of gossip can offer many benefits. Personal growth, healthier relationships, a positive mindset, and a more uplifting environment for everyone involved are among the advantages. When you choose not to engage in negative chatter, you contribute to a culture that celebrates positive communication, encourages empathy, and reduces unnecessary drama and conflict. It takes a lot of self-discipline to choose not to gossip, but doing so will enrich our lives with deeper, more genuine conversations.

Aim to use your words to contribute something useful, meaningful, or enriching. One might share some helpful information, discuss a hobby, or share jokes. A few examples of topics you can fruitfully discuss include cooking, baking, fitness, wellness, books, travel, movies, stress-relief, movies, gardening, volunteering, self-care, sports, shopping, television, magazines, design, science, art, hobbies, philosophy, and parenting.

Kindness is *choosing* to speak about things that are positive, fun, helpful, lighthearted, and amusing simply because you want to uplift the other person. Try to focus on conversations of enrichment and empowerment. Let your words reflect compassion rather than criticism, and be willing to spread light instead of negativity. When we choose to lift those around us, we change the world. Create an atmosphere where people feel encouraged to be their authentic selves without fear of judgment. This positive reinforcement can not only boost your self-esteem but also strengthen community bonds and even inspire others to be kinder.

THE GIFT OF YOUR PRESENCE

Sometimes, just being there is the greatest gift. Time—the rhythm of your life, the hours that embellish your days, and the moments shared with those you love. In today's fast-paced world, where each day demands more from us than we have time for, the hours have become invaluable. Generously offering your most prized gift to someone is a heartfelt way to show kindness.

Whether you enjoy time bonding with a family member, help a coworker on a project, spend time with a friend, or volunteer at a local charity, giving someone moments of your day is a thoughtful way to show them that they matter. It conveys that you value that person and their needs. This modest form of kindness can have a positive impact on someone's life while also enriching your own life with time spent meaningfully.

Simply being present for a conversation and truly listening can make a world of difference. Life hums and buzzes with constant distractions, and it can be easy to overlook the importance of actively listening to others when they speak to you. Gifting kindness means giving your time and your full attention. Instead of looking at your phone, thinking about something you have going on, interrupting, or rushing to offer a response, listen to others attentively. Being there and listening with empathy can show that you care about their thoughts, feelings, and experiences. It can make people feel valued and respected.

SPREADING JOY THROUGH KINDNESS

Stir and spread moments of grace and gladness with a tiny habit of kindness. Like untamed wildflowers, random acts of kindness bloom freely, unexpectedly, and naturally, brightening the path of all who pass. They give the traveler a glimmer of beauty and hope amid the difficulties they may be experiencing on their journey.

A very rewarding way to practice being kind is through random acts of kindness. These small, selfless gestures can include giving a nice compliment, holding the door open for someone, or paying for a stranger's coffee or lunch. These spontaneous acts don't have to be elaborate or costly; sometimes, the smallest actions have the greatest impact. No matter what your financial situation may be, within you, you possess great wealth in the form of kindness. Give it to others open-handedly. Saying hello with a smile, offering words of encouragement, and helping someone carry a heavy load are all ways we can spread kindness in our everyday routines.

What makes these gentle gestures so wonderful is that they not only help others but also make us feel good, reinforcing the positive cycle of kindness. The joy you seek in life is not found after a lifelong quest. It is experienced in everyday moments when your heart and soul feel aligned, at peace, and content. Making kindness a part of your routine is a subtle practice with fulfilling, joy-boosting power.

Random acts of kindness toward your family are just as valuable as they are for strangers. Taking care of your loved ones and doing things that make them happy are acts of compassion. They depend on you for affection and care. Your generosity can deeply impact the quality of your family's life. Use kindness as a tool to help create more moments of cheer in their day. You have the power to make those who hold your heart feel happy, loved, and special. Cherish this power and treat them well.

I'm sure you already have many lovely ways of offering thoughtful gestures, but still, I'd love to share a few of my favorite heartwarming ways. Write your own list and start stirring sweet acts of kindness into your daily life. Never underestimate the power of even the smallest deeds of compassion. Always be ready to lend a hand, to boost, and to gift gentleness where it is least expected.

Perhaps you may change someone's life. Perhaps they will be inspired to change someone else's. The world will always need more kindness. Let your heart guide you to lift someone's spirits through a small act of goodness, for in the end, you will be rising from within, too.

BREWING KINDNESS: SMALL ACTS TO SPREAD JOY

- ♥ Make a cup of tea for a friend or family member.
- ♥ Dedicate a day to celebrating yourself. Buy flowers and a treat. Sip tea and take in the moment as you write down three things that you love about yourself.
- ♥ Take groceries for someone you are visiting.

- Send flowers to a friend.
- Teach someone a skill you are good at.
- Give someone nourishing tea and a good book.
- Inspire someone by texting them a motivational quote.
- Bake a cake for your coworkers.
- Enjoy a fun and playful experience with a friend or family member.
- Donate gently used towels or blankets to a shelter.
- Cook a meal for a friend or family member.
- Leave snacks and refreshments for delivery drivers.
- Mail someone a beautiful, handwritten card filled with gratitude.
- Look in the mirror, smile, and say 3 positive things about yourself.
- Donate a toy to a child in need.
- Instead of buying yourself a new outfit you don't really need, use that money to buy a gift for someone who is going through a difficult time.
- Let someone go in front of you in the queue.
- Leave a positive review for a local business online.
- Spend some free time enjoying a hobby that brings you joy.
- Send an encouraging email to a coworker.
- Donate a book to your local library.

- Shop local and support small businesses.
- Take time to play a game with a child in your life.
- Tell your family members how much you love and appreciate them.
- Write uplifting messages on sticky notes and leave them where others will find them.
- Leave a generous tip for someone.
- Celebrate yourself or a loved one by donating something in their honor to a person in need.
- Leave quarters at the laundromat or vending machine.
- Sign up to do volunteer work in your local community.
- Make and send a care package to someone who needs it.
- Say good morning. Say goodnight.
- Plant a tree or flowers.
- Stick little love notes or gentle reminders to yourself in different spots around your home to brighten your day.
- Donate to a charity.
- Bake cookies for a friend.
- Hold the door open for someone.
- Make a cup of tea for your colleagues.
- Tell a loved one that you are grateful to have them in your life.
- Give up your seat to someone elderly, disabled, or pregnant.

- Let a fellow driver merge into your lane.
- Buy coffee for the person behind you in line.
- Send a kind text message to three people you care about to let them know you are thinking about them.
- Run an errand for a busy family member.
- Put your phone away while in the company of others.
- Be an active listener when someone speaks to you.
- Smile and say hello to people you may pass every day.
- Write your partner a list of things you love about them.
- Instead of buying coffee or tea, donate that money one day a week to help provide clean drinking water to someone in need.
- On your birthday or a special occasion, bake cupcakes and take them to a homeless shelter, food bank, or anywhere you would like to spread sweetness on the happiest of days.
- Take a moment to pause for beauty, savoring life's simple pleasures, fully present. You might consider sipping a calming cup of tea, wandering through a blooming garden, or sitting in stillness to breathe in the fragrance of flowers.
- Speak to your family with kind, tender words.
- Give someone a teapot of gentle reminders. Write little notes of kindness on small pieces of paper and place

them all in a teapot to give to someone
to warm their heart and brighten their day.

    Let us be artisans of kindness, displaying our hearts through acts so beautiful and endearing that they leave a lasting, positive impact on others' lives. Let us be spring's first bloom after winter's long stillness. Be the light in darkness. The warmth on a cold day. Let us remind ourselves and others that love is everywhere in the world, and we are not alone.

26

The Beauty You Almost Missed

In Prague, I set out on a morning walk to practice mindfulness and soak in the morning light. There is something about this charming city that inspires me to be present, to be mindful of the beauty and magic that surrounds me in this fairytale.

Walking in nature allows us to get some fresh air and clear our minds. Admiring the splendor of nature and the way that everything comes together so harmoniously is truly heartening. It can take our minds off sources of stress and lighten our spirits with a sense of peace.

Upon entering the exquisite garden, enchanted with beauty and life, I remind myself to see, hear, touch, taste, smell, and explore this place to get the most out of it. My eyes are immediately drawn to the shimmering dance of light upon the calm, flowing water. The sun's brilliant reflection transforms the water into something celestial. The scene is spellbinding. The place is alive with verve and energy.

The serene sound of the trees blowing with the wind greets my ears and soothes my soul. The birds chirp tenderly, creating a sweet song. These heartening sounds come together melodiously, creating music so calming that nothing else can quite compare. The cool breeze gently touches my cheek and plays with my hair. I can almost taste the freshness of the air on my tongue.

Glorious trees and lush greenery adorn the place. Sculpted hedges lavishly ornament the garden. My! Such grandeur exists in nature! Bright tulips in red, pink, and white stand merrily. I look around, my heart blooming with contentment. A woodsy odor mingled with a faint whiff of flowers and water greets my nose; the refreshing smell of nature. At once, I am mesmerized.

I thoroughly explore the park by contemplating how all this beauty came together to create this stunning masterpiece. I wonder about the birds' journey. I find myself dreaming up the story of the trees that have been standing strong for hundreds of years. With quiet rapture and curiosity, I breathe in the moment, and with each breath, I take in the magnificence that surrounds me. I realize that joy grows wild in nature, and if we just take time to slow down and notice it with mindfulness and presence, we can actually *feel* it. I dwell a little longer until I realize that it is time for a tranquil moment of tea at the café.

——— ✦ ———

Wander often, wander slowly, making sure that you notice the beauty you almost missed. If you see a rainbow, take a moment to marvel at its magic. If you see a butterfly, follow it, seeing its beauty and observing its path. Like the child who is an expert in embracing the present, we too must reconnect with our inner child. She pauses to examine a ladybug, gazes at the cloud shaped like a cat, and is mesmerized by the smallest details that we grownups take for granted. In her, there is no hurry, no regret, no plan—only the profound intrigue with the moment.

Observe her attention to the present—blooming with joy and fascination. She happily notices the beauty already there and does not ask, "What is next?" Instead, with true enthusiasm, she may ask, "What is this?" And, it is in that question of the child that we may find the key to presence: a passion to engage with the present with an open heart and with wonder.

If you wake up to a new day, live it to the fullest by meeting each moment as it is. With all that each day demands from us, we might have so much on our plate that we may forget to pause and notice the beauty, joy, and richness of the present. It may slip by unnoticed amid our daily loads, our past regrets, and our future worries. Essential to a more intentional lifestyle, living in the present means taking time to see the wonder you nearly overlooked.

Pause for life's sweet moments by slowing down, appreciating the warmth of daily comforts, and cherishing life's fleeting beauty. Celebrate the small moments in each hour, in each day, and be present to experience the good things that life gifts you fully. Focus on basking in the sunshine of today.

If you often find yourself thinking about the past or wishing for the future, this is an opportunity to learn to dwell in gardens that are blooming now. Living in the present allows you to savor the beauty and sweetness nestled within the simplest details of each day. This requires a shift in mindset, one that prioritizes mindfulness over multitasking and just existing, rather than constantly keeping busy. While leading a productive lifestyle and planning for the future are important, it's also essential to realize that life is happening right now, in this moment.

Today is more special than any other day, for it is the only time that truly belongs to you. Happiness is not in the past, nor can you travel back in time to find it. No one really knows what tomorrow may hold. Yet, today, happiness could very well happen. Immerse yourself in the joys offered by the present hour. Enjoy the bloom of each moment.

Learning to experience greater peace, joy, and satisfaction with life entails putting the past behind you, releasing worries about the days ahead, and being fully engaged in the here and now. While it is okay to reminisce about happy memories every so often, it is better to build new memories of love and joy today. Every minute spent reflecting on the past is a chance at fun lost today. The only time that is guaranteed is the present. Denying oneself the simple pleasure of fully embracing each passing moment would be a great injustice.

Taking a mindful pause can be the first step to being present. Slowing your rhythm can certainly feel counterintuitive when we are expected to work quickly, stay busy, and increase productivity. Nevertheless, it is important to slow down and take a break, as this pause can help us reconnect with ourselves and our surroundings. Finding a moment to breathe and see the beauty around you can be an uplifting way to recharge when the day starts to feel a little overwhelming. When you allow yourself a few minutes to relax, inhale, and exhale, you can feel inspired to open yourself up to the joy and wonder that surrounds you.

Free yourself from what was and what's yet to come. Allow yourself to bring your full attention and all of your emotions to today. The only time that you are guaranteed is this very moment. It is precious. Today, you are breathing. Today, your heart is beating. Nurture your heart and soul in the present, dancing to the rhythm of today.

SAVORING THE PRESENT

How strange it is that we are so often consumed by thoughts of what may be in the future that we fail to settle into the present. Set your mind and yourself free by letting go of unnecessary worries or plans about the future. Practice substituting unhelpful thoughts with simple ideas for making the most of today, creating space for joy now. Taking what you have for granted today with hopes of having something better tomorrow would be unfair to your own heart. Appreciate what you have been blessed with right now, gathering the flowers today gives.

Nurture a habit of basking in the present. Mindfulness is key to tuning in to what is happening right now, to what belongs to you today. It is a rather enlightening practice that encourages us to be aware of our thoughts, feelings, sensations, and surroundings. Accept what is currently occurring without judgment, but with a sense of curiosity. This can help us cultivate greater awareness and connection to the gift of now.

Whether you are eating a meal, taking a bath, or having a conversation, experience common, everyday activities thoroughly so you can get a greater sense of contentment from them. As you pause and notice, you unlock the beauty in everyday experiences, and with time, your heart grows fuller with appreciation.

IN THIS MOMENT: BEAUTY, JOY, AND LOVE

You don't have to stay stuck in scarcity—you can choose gratitude and abundance. Remember that the contentment you are seeking is already there, waiting to be noticed and relished. From the warmth in your heart upon receiving a hug from a loved one to the soothing sounds of nature, every moment in life is full of potential for joy and gratitude. Thoroughly engrossing yourself in these moments is essential for achieving true, enduring happiness.

With all its beauty and charm, the world is open for you to see, hear, touch, taste, smell, and discover. You have the privilege of experiencing all the splendors with your entire being. Allow yourself to be cradled by little joys. This is how you truly embrace the practice of dwelling fully in this moment.

When you are in your garden, simply admiring the bubblegum-pink and periwinkle hydrangeas is not enough. Take a mindful pause. With your eyes, capture a picture of the gentle clusters, where bold, full blossoms gather like soft clouds, cradling smaller, delicate florets nestled within. Open your ears to the sound of the breeze blowing against the clusters of star-shaped blossoms. Feel the softness of the dainty petals with your fingers.

Breathe in the refreshing scents of the world unfolding around you, identifying the medley of fragrances in the air. At the zenith of its beauty, the hydrangeas are a sight to be admired. Explore this scene by questioning how its environment affects its growth and colors, or wondering how the plant feels when you touch it softly. Experience everything around you with all of your senses to live each moment more deeply.

Sip the beauty around you. Slow down, hug the present, and find delight and delicate wonder in the little things. Make time to enjoy the blessings that grace your day. It is the humble but heartfelt experiences that add happiness and meaning to our lives. When you breathe in the beauty around you, you appreciate a cup of tea in the morning, the warmth of sunshine on your skin, and the colors of a sunset. These often-overlooked pleasures are what make life lovely.

When we intentionally pause to experience the simple pleasures, we discover that life is not just about big achievements or grand experiences; it's about the quiet, everyday miracles that make us feel alive. Savor the tiny sips of joy. Take time to notice the beauty already there.

Be present in your relationships. Spending time with family and friends is an agreeable way to glorify the hour. Living in the moment also means nurturing love and creating deeper connections by being more present with others. Strong relationships have a positive impact on joy. It may, however, be difficult to achieve until you start putting away your phone and truly dedicating time to spending with others.

In the hustle of everyday life, we may find ourselves rushing through interactions. Remind yourself to be present when in the company of loved ones by offering these moments in their honor, being attentive during conversations, and staying engaged. Listening, showing empathy, and giving someone your time by truly being there without distractions can help you nurture more caring, warm, and rewarding relationships.

> **SIP OF INSPIRATION**
>
> Today, be fully there with someone you love. Enjoy stories, laughter, and simply being together. Did you notice or learn anything about the person?

Life is happening right now, and each day holds immeasurable worth. Embrace each breath with gratitude and intention, letting it fill you with contentment, calm, and a sense of wholeness. Every moment holds the potential for beauty, joy, love, and connection. Open your heart to life's richness and delight by savoring the present. Seize the many small opportunities to maximize happiness in everyday life by harnessing the power of mindful habits of tea and joy.

Daily Habits, Warm Sips, Joyful Living

The world is your wonderland, with adventure at every turn. Today may be cloudy and gloomy, but it shows another lovely side of this world and of life. The sky looks like a glimmering candlelight, casting light on us all. The magnificent trees, looking greener against the gray background, no longer have to be thirsty.

With your eyes, you see darkness for miles ahead on the drenched road. But the plants dance merrily along twirling leaves dripping with raindrops. Animals come out to play in the rain. The earth derives comfort from the shade and water after the warm, thirsty days of sunshine. Nature rejoices during this happy occasion.

You roll down your window just a little. Cold, refreshing drops of water sprinkle from the sky and kiss your face. It feels like the dew from the roses of heaven has fallen from the clouds and touched your face.

Rainy days are a bore, you say? Drizzly days allow you to experience the world dreamily. Although tea and solitude make the finest companions on a rainy afternoon, it is a pleasure to indulge in something different now and then. Go home and put on your fluffy socks, because fluffy socks are a lifestyle choice. Sink into your comfy chair with a warm mug of hot cocoa, foamy with cream and slowly melting marshmallows. Truly immerse yourself in an hour of cozy contentment.

Look out the window, and be still so you can hear the whisper of the rain chimes. Watch the droplets trickle down and wash your window, your home, your little world. As rain pours from the sky, it showers the earth. It rinses off muck, washes away impurities, and leaves a gleaming environment for a new day, a new beginning, and new hope.

Life slows down for you a little on rainy days, giving you moments to enjoy at home thoroughly. You get to bond with your favorite people and get closer and cozier than you otherwise could. Let's not let another moment slip by—grab your softest blankets, snuggle in close, and press play on something feel-good. Joy blooms on quiet nights in, wrapped in warmth and surrounded by the ones who make home feel like magic.

Before long, the weather lets up. A glimpse of the sun can be seen through the elephant-shaped clouds, and then, you see a magical projection between the sky and earth, a rainbow. It brings colors of optimism into your life. Time fetches the resplendent sun, and the murky clouds slowly disperse. The sun's warm rays reach out to you as though touching your forehead with a comforting hand, like a mother soothing her child. Be sure to catch the sunlight while it lasts.

Every day is wondrous in its own special way. Make a habit of viewing each experience with a positive outlook and an open heart, and you may discover that there is so much to be grateful for. Let the world bloom around you. Look upon every situation as an opportunity for growth and happiness. Life is a quest, and you must search for beauty in everything. You must choose bright, cheerful colors and use them to paint a beautiful, little world so that you can live with more intention, love, and contentment.

Joy grows wild in the places you pass through without noticing—in the layers of ordinary life that can reveal themselves only when you slow down enough to look. It's in the pauses between destinations. It's in the habits we return to. It's in the noticing. Joy is all around us. Indeed, there is much beauty and calm present in our daily lives. They may be little or hidden in the smallest details. Take time to notice the good things.

Whether it's the first sip of something warm when the air turns cold, sunlight streaming through the window and giving life a gilded glow, or the enchanting fragrance of a rose, numerous moments in each day are worthy of your attention. These moments are all gifts, but only if you are present enough to notice them. Be grateful for the good things in life. Happiness will be in your heart.

Hurry along. Your adventure filled with tea, love, and gratitude begins *now*.

Where Joy Grows Wild

Is there a place where joy grows wild? This is the very question that I asked at the beginning of my journey when I set out not in search of love or reinvention, but for something gentler. I sought the kind of joy that isn't grand or glittering—but rather, the kind that lingers quietly, like steam rising softly from a cup of tea, like a comforting scent in the air.

Openheartedly, I wandered through tearooms around San Francisco, New York, England, Istanbul, and beyond—and in each place, I found small, persistent joys. It was in the rhythm of footsteps along wet cobblestone streets adorned with flower stalls and cafés. It was in the air, faintly smelling of earth and espresso. It was hidden in a cup of Earl Grey cradled in the cold hands of a mother having tea with her daughters by the glow of candlelight. It was everywhere that the ordinary became beautiful simply because I took the time to notice.

But here's what I didn't expect: that the wildest joy—the kind that doesn't need tending, the kind that *is*—was waiting for me right at home. It grows in the kitchen bathed in sunlight. In the hum of the heater on cold mornings. In the familiar clink of my favorite old mug, the one with the faint crack on the handle. In the morning routine that begins my day. In the little habits that brighten up life. In the scent of our linens, the smell of bread baking in the oven, the rhythm of sweeping the floor, the sound of nothing when everything is still.

Home is not always peaceful or perfect. But it is what I know best. It is colorful with memories, warmed by love and tenderness. Here, joy doesn't need to be discovered—it just needs to be *noticed*.

And so, it turns out, joy doesn't bloom only in far-off places. Nor does it just dwell in curated moments. It grows wild where we live our lives. It grows freely in repetition, in habits, in presence, in the moments of beauty and contentment that we intentionally create.

And much like wildflowers, joy doesn't ask for much—only that we leave room for it to grow. So yes, there is a place where joy grows wild. It's in our hearts, it's in our minds, it's right where you are—in the quiet corners of home. It's in all the places that know your laughter, your tears, your story. It's in the life you've built slowly, one small practice and one tiny habit at a time. And perhaps the wildest joy of all is realizing... you never had to go far to find it.

Beep. Beep. Beep. The oven's timer sings its cheerful tune—the chocolate chip cookies are ready. As I eagerly pull open the oven door, a divine scent of ooey-gooey chocolate, golden butter, and sweet sugar fills the air. I breathe in the heartwarming smell, slip my hand into the tea-themed oven mitt, and lift the pan with care. I place the cookies on a cupcake-shaped plate and happily set it on the table for my family to enjoy. With a pink, heart-shaped cup of tea warming my fingers and loved ones gathered near, I am filled with a beautiful truth. Joy blooms from the heart like gorgeous wildflowers bathed in morning light, brushing vibrant color onto the quiet canvas of unwritten afternoons. It reminds us that life's simplest moments hold the deepest beauty, and that empowering habits and love are the light that helps everything grow.

About the Author

Zakiyya Rosebelle is an author and founder of Teatimely, a lifestyle brand devoted to joyful living that offers books and thoughtfully curated resources to help you bring more beauty and intention to everyday life. Her insights and her expertise have been featured in leading publications.

Zakiyya created The Tea & Joy Method to offer a softer, more sustainable approach to personal growth. It's a daily practice that centers on tea, calm, gratitude, self-care, and connection. This gentle system draws on tea rituals and small, mindful habits to create a calmer, more joyful way of living.

For anyone feeling overwhelmed, seeking peace, or wanting to savor more delight in daily life, this method offers simple practices to slow down, reconnect with what matters, and design joy in everyday moments. In the expanded, hardcover edition of *Daily Habits of Tea and Joy*, readers are invited to go deeper into the Teatimely Habits Method—a unique, ritualized habit-building framework.

After completing this book, she created *Daily Habits of Joy: A 90-Day Gratitude & Self-Care Guided Journal*. It offers simple, meaningful prompts to nurture habits of joy, support self-care, encourage calm, and notice the good in each day.

When she's not writing, Zakiyya can usually be found with a warm cup of tea, practicing intentional living and habits of joy, and finding beauty in life's quieter moments with loved ones.

———— ✦✦✦ ————

CONTINUE NURTURING YOUR JOY
WITH A FREE COMPANION EXPERIENCE

A soothing guided meditation + heartfelt journaling prompts to help you unwind and reflect.

Download yours at: *Teatimely.com/joy*

www.ingramcontent.com/pod-product-compliance
Lightning Source LLC
LaVergne TN
LVHW091719070526
838199LV00050B/2460